W9-DBO-353

Holiness

Its Nature, Hindrances, Difficulties and Roots

J.C. Ryle

Holiness

J.C. Ryle

(1816–1900)

10 Publishing
a division of 10 ofthose.com

Unless otherwise stated, Scripture quotations are taken from
THE HOLY BIBLE, NEW INTERNATIONAL VERSION (Anglicised
Edition). Copyright © 1979, 1984, 2011 by Biblica (formerly
International Bible Society). Used by permission of Hodder &
Stoughton Publishers. All rights reserved. 'NIV' is a registered
trademark of Biblica. UK trademark number 1448790.

Scripture quotations marked KJV are taken from the
King James Version of the Bible

Holiness first published 1879. This abridged edition (and with
most Bible texts updated to the NIV Bible) published 2014 by
10Publishing
Reprinted 2016

British Library Cataloguing in Publication Data
A record for this book is available from the British Library

ISBN: 978-1-909611-80-1

Designed and typeset by Pete Barnsley (Creative Hoot)
Printed in Denmark by Nørhaven

10Publishing, a division of 10ofthose.com
Unit C, Tomlinson Road, Leyland, Lancashire, PR25 2DY, England

Email: info@10ofthose.com
Website: www.10ofthose.com

Contents

Publisher's Note

We are delighted to publish this book, which continues to be a much-loved classic. It is striking that, though originally written more than a hundred years ago, the book is still as relevant as ever today. As you read it, you will be reminded of the essential need for all Christians to be not only vigilant in our personal holiness but also active in pursuing this goal to which we are called. Ryle's words will both inspire and challenge.

Over the years, many versions of *Holiness* have been published. While J.C. Ryle orginally wrote twenty papers that were combined to make a book, we have chosen to produce this abridged version of what we consider to be the most important and pertinent chapters. Our hope in publishing this more accessible edition is that it will appeal to those who might otherwise not pick it up and benefit from its timeless wisdom.

The other distinction of our edition is that we have amended the Bible texts that Ryle quotes to the latest NIV version, unless the original KING JAMES VERSION is better suited in the context. As most readers will be familiar with and accustomed to the wording of the NIV, we trust this will be a helpful change.

Author's Preface

The volume now in the reader's hands is an enlarged edition of a small work which appeared two years ago, and has been kindly received by the Christian public. The present volume contains so much additional matter that it is double the size of the predecessor. In fact, the work is half new.

I venture to think that the papers contained in this volume will be found helpful by all who take an interest in the subject of scriptural holiness. I am much mistaken if they do not throw broad light on the real nature of holiness, and the temptations and difficulties which all must expect who follow it. Above all, I hope they will help to bring forward the grand truth that union with Christ is the root of holiness, and will show young believers what immense encouragement Jesus Christ holds out to all who strive to be holy.

Concerning the present position of the whole subject of holiness among English Christians, the older I grow the more I am convinced that there is a most painfully low standard of living among many in the land who claim to be Christians. But, at the same time, I am increasingly convinced that the zealous efforts of some well-meaning persons to promote a higher standard of spiritual life are often not 'according to knowledge', and are really calculated to do more harm than good. Let me explain what I mean.

It is easy to get crowds together for what are called 'higher life' and 'consecration' meetings. Anyone knows that who has watched human nature and read descriptions of American camp-meetings and studied the curious phenomena of the 'religious affections'. Sensational and exciting addresses by strange preachers or by women, loud singing, hot rooms, crowded tents, the constant sight of strong semi-religious feeling in the faces of all around you for several days, late hours, long protracted meetings, public profession of experience – all this kind of thing is very interesting at the time and seems to do good. But is the good real, deeply rooted, solid lasting? That is the point. And I should like to ask a few questions about it.

Do those who attend these meetings become more holy, meek, unselfish, kind, good-tempered, self-denying and Christ-like at home? Do they become more content with their position in life, and more free from restless craving after something different from that which God has given them? Do fathers, mothers, husbands and other relatives and friends find them more pleasant and easy to live with? Can they enjoy a quiet Sunday and quiet means of grace without noise, heat and excitement? Above all, do they grow in charity, and especially in charity towards those who do not agree with them in every jot and tittle of their religion?

These are serious and searching questions and deserve serious consideration. I hope I am as anxious to promote real practical holiness in the land as anyone. I admire and willingly acknowledge the zeal and earnestness of many with whom I cannot co-operate who are trying to promote it. But I cannot withhold a growing suspicion that the great 'mass-meetings' of the present day, for the ostensible object of promoting spiritual life, do not tend to promote private home religion, private Bible-reading, private prayer, private usefulness and private walking with God. If they are of any real value, they ought to make people better husbands and wives and fathers and mothers and sons and daughters and brothers and sisters and servants. But I should like to have clear proofs that they do. I only know it is far easier to be a Christian among singing, praying, sympathizing Christians in a public room than to be a consistent Christian in a quiet, retired, out-of-the-way, uncongenial home. The first position is one in which there is a great deal of nature to help us: the second is one which cannot be well filled without grace. But, alas, many talk nowadays about '*consecration*', while they seem to be ignorant of the first principle of the oracles of God about '*conversion*'.

I close this preface with the sorrowful feeling that probably some who read it will not agree with me. To the young especially I can see that the great gatherings of the so-called 'spiritual life' movement are sure to be attractive. They naturally like zeal and stir and enthusiasm, and they say, 'Where is the harm?' Be it so: we must agree to differ. When I was young as they are, perhaps I should have thought as they do. When they are old as I am, they will very likely agree with me.

To each and all of my readers, I say in conclusion, let us exercise charity in our judgements of one another. Towards those who think holiness is to be promoted by the modern, so-called 'spiritual life' movement, I feel nothing but charity. If they do good,

I am thankful. Towards myself and those who agree with me, I ask them to feel charity in return. The last day will show who is right and who is wrong. In the meantime, I am quite certain that to exhibit bitterness and coldness towards those who cannot conscientiously work with us is to prove ourselves very ignorant of real holiness.

J.C. Ryle

1879

1

Sin

'... sin is lawlessness'

(1 John 3:4)

He who wishes to attain right views about Christian *holiness* must begin by examining the vast and solemn subject of *sin*. He must dig down very *low* if he would build *high*. A mistake here is most mischievous. Wrong views about holiness are generally traceable to wrong views about human corruption. I make no apology for beginning this volume of messages about *holiness* by making some plain statements about *sin*.

The plain truth is that a right understanding of *sin* lies at the root of all saving Christianity. Without it, such doctrines as justification, conversion and sanctification are 'words and names' which convey no meaning to the mind. The first thing, therefore, that God does when He makes anyone a new creature in Christ is to send light into his heart and show him that he is a *guilty sinner*. The material creation in Genesis began with 'light', and so also does the spiritual creation. God 'made his light shine in our hearts' by the work of the Holy Spirit – and then spiritual life begins (2 Cor. 4:6).

Dim or indistinct views of sin are the origin of most of the errors, heresies and false doctrines of the present day. If a man does not realize the dangerous nature of his *soul's disease* you cannot wonder if he is content with false or imperfect *remedies*. I believe that one of the chief needs of the contemporary church has been, and is, clearer, fuller teaching about sin.

1. I will begin the subject by supplying some definition of sin. We are all, of course, familiar with the terms 'sin' and 'sinners'. We talk frequently of 'sin' being in the world, and of men committing 'sins'. But what do we mean by these terms and phrases? Do we really know? I fear there is much mental confusion and haziness on this point. Let me try, as briefly as possible, to supply an answer.

'Sin', speaking generally, is, as the ninth Article of our church declares:

> the fault and corruption of the Nature of every man, that naturally is engendered of the offspring of Adam; whereby man is very far gone from original righteousness, and is of his own nature inclined to evil, so that the flesh lusteth always contrary to the Spirit; and therefore in every person born into this world, it deserveth God's wrath and damnation.

Sin is that vast moral disease which affects the whole human race of every rank and class and name and nation and people and tongue;

a disease from which there never was but one born of woman that was free. Need I say, that One was Christ Jesus the Lord?

I say, furthermore, that 'a sin', to speak more particularly, *consists in doing, saying, thinking or imagining anything that is not in perfect conformity with the mind and law of God*. 'Sin' in short, as the Scripture says, 'is lawlessness' (1 John 3:4). The slightest outward or inward departure from absolute mathematical parallelism with God's revealed will and character constitutes a sin, and at once makes us guilty in God's sight.

Of course, I need not tell anyone who reads their Bible with attention that a man may break God's law in *heart* and *thought*, when there is no overt and visible act of wickedness. Our Lord has settled that point beyond dispute in the Sermon on the Mount (Matt. 5:21–28). Even a poet of our own has truly said that 'one may smile, and smile, and be a villain'.

Again, I need not tell a careful student of the New Testament that there are sins of *omission* as well as *commission*, and that we sin, as our Prayer Book justly reminds us, by 'leaving undone the things we ought to do', as really as by 'doing the things we ought not to do'. The solemn words of our Master in the Gospel of Matthew place this point also beyond dispute. It is there written: 'Depart from me, you who are cursed, into the eternal fire ... For I was hungry and you gave me nothing to eat, I was thirsty and you gave me nothing to drink' (Matt. 25:41,42).

I do think it necessary in these times to remind my readers that a man may commit sin and yet be ignorant of it, and imagine himself innocent – when he is guilty. I fail to see any scriptural warrant for the modern assertion that 'Sin is not sin *to us* – until we discern it and are conscious of it'. On the contrary, in the fourth and fifth chapters of that unduly neglected book, Leviticus, and in the fifteenth of Numbers, I find Israel distinctly taught that there were *sins of ignorance* which rendered people unclean, and needed atonement (Lev. 4; 5:14–19; Num. 15:25–29). And I find our Lord expressly teaching that the servant who *knows not* his master's will and 'does things deserving punishment' was not excused on account of his ignorance, but was 'beaten' or punished (Luke 12:48). We will do well to remember that when we make our own miserably imperfect knowledge and consciousness the measure of our sinfulness, we are on very dangerous ground. A deeper study of Leviticus might do us much good.

2. Concerning the *origin* and *source* of this vast moral disease called 'sin', I am afraid that the views of many professing Christians on this point are sadly defective and unsound. I dare not pass it by. Let us, then, have it fixed down in our minds that the sinfulness of man does not begin from *without* but from *within*. It is not the result of bad training in early years. It is not picked up from bad companions and bad examples – as some weak Christians are too fond of saying. No! It is a family disease, which we all inherit from our first parents, Adam and Eve, and with which we are born.

Created in the image of God, innocent and righteous at first, our parents fell from original righteousness, and became sinful and corrupt. And from that day to this, all men and women are born in the image of fallen Adam and Eve, and inherit a heart and nature inclined to evil: '... sin entered the world through one man'; 'Flesh gives birth to flesh'; '... we were *by nature* deserving of wrath'; 'The mind governed by the flesh is hostile to God'; '... it is from within, out of a person's heart, that evil thoughts come – sexual immorality' and the like (Rom. 5:12; John 3:6; Eph. 2:3, italics mine; Rom. 8:7; Mark 7:21).

The fairest child, who has entered life this year and become the sunbeam of a family, is not, as his mother perhaps fondly calls him, a little 'angel' or a little 'innocent', but a little 'sinner'. Alas! As that boy or girl lies smiling and crowing in their cradle, that little infant carries the seeds of every kind of wickedness in its heart! Only watch it carefully, as it grows in stature and its mind develops, and you will soon detect in it an incessant tendency to that which is bad, and a backwardness to do that which is good. You will see in it the buds and germs of deceit, evil temper, selfishness, self-will, obstinacy, greediness, envy, jealousy and passion – which, if indulged and let alone, will shoot up with painful rapidity.

Who taught the child these things? Where did he learn them? The Bible alone can answer these questions. Of all the foolish things that parents say about their children, there is none worse than the common saying: 'My son has a good heart at the bottom. He is not what he ought to be, but he has fallen into bad hands. Public schools are bad places – the teachers neglect the boys. Yet he has a good heart at the bottom.' The truth, unhappily, is diametrically the other way. The first cause of all sin lies in the natural corruption of the boy's own heart – and not in public schools!

3. Concerning the *extent* of this vast moral disease called 'sin', let us beware that we make no mistake. The only safe ground is that which is laid for us in Scripture. '... every inclination of the thoughts of the human heart' is by nature 'evil', and that 'all the time'. 'The heart is deceitful above all things and beyond cure ' (Gen. 6:5; Jer. 17:9). Sin is a disease which pervades and runs through every part of our moral constitution, and every faculty of our minds. The *understanding*, the *affections*, the *reasoning powers*, the *will* are all more or less infected. Even the *conscience* is so blinded that it cannot be depended on as a sure guide, and is as likely to lead men wrong as right, unless it is enlightened by the Holy Spirit. In short, 'From the sole of your foot to the top of your head there is no soundness – only wounds and bruises and open sores' (Isa. 1:6). The disease may be *veiled* under a thin covering of courtesy, politeness, good manners and outward decorum – but it lies deep down in the constitution!

I admit fully that man has many grand and noble faculties left about him, and that in arts and sciences and literature he shows immense capacity. But the fact still remains that in spiritual things he is utterly 'dead' and has no natural knowledge, or love, or fear of God. His *best* things are so interwoven and intermingled with *corruption* that the contrast only brings out into sharper relief the truth and extent of the Fall. That one and the same creature should be in some things so high, and in others so low; so great, and yet so little; so noble, and yet so base; so grand in his conception and execution of material things, and yet so grovelling and debased in his affections; that he should be able to plan and erect buildings like the pyramids in Egypt and the Parthenon at Athens, and yet worship vile gods and goddesses and birds and beasts and creeping things; that he should be able to produce histories like that of Thucydides, and yet be a slave to abominable vices like those described in the first chapter of the epistle to the Romans – all this is a sore puzzle to those who sneer at 'God's Word' and scoff at us as *bibliolaters*.

But it is a knot that we can untie, with the Bible in our hands. We can acknowledge that man has all the marks of a majestic temple about him, a temple in which God once dwelt – but a temple which is now in utter ruins, a temple in which a shattered window here and a doorway there and a column there still give some faint idea of the magnificence of the original design, but a temple which from end to end has lost its glory and fallen from its high estate. And we say that nothing solves the complicated problem of man's condition, but the doctrine of *original* or *birth-sin*, and the crushing effects of the Fall.

Let us remember, beside this, that every part of the world bears testimony to the fact that *sin is the universal disease of all mankind*. Search the globe from east to west and from pole to pole; search every nation of every climate in the four quarters of the earth; search every rank and class in our own country, from the highest to the lowest – and under every circumstance and condition, the report will be always the same. The remotest islands in the Pacific Ocean, completely separate from Europe, Asia, Africa and America, beyond the reach alike of Oriental luxury and Western arts and literature, islands inhabited by people ignorant of books, money, steam engines, uncontaminated by the vices of modern civilization – these very islands have always been found, when first discovered, the abode of the vilest forms of lust, cruelty, deceit and superstition. If the inhabitants have known nothing else, they have always known how to sin! Everywhere the human heart is naturally 'deceitful above all things and beyond cure' (Jer. 17:9).

For my part, I know no stronger proof of the inspiration of Genesis and the Mosaic account of the origin of man, than the *power, extent* and *universality* of sin. Grant that mankind have all sprung from one pair, and that this pair fell (as Gen. 3 tells us), and the state of human nature everywhere is easily accounted for. Deny it, as many do, and you are at once involved in inexplicable difficulties. In a word, the *uniformity and universality of human corruption* supply one of the most unanswerable instances of the enormous 'difficulties of infidelity'.

After all, I am convinced that the greatest proof of the extent and power of sin is the *pertinacity* with which it cleaves to man even after he is converted and has become the subject of the Holy Spirit's operations. To use the language of the ninth Article: '... this infection of nature doth remain – yea, in them that are regenerated ...' So deeply planted are the roots of human corruption that even after we are born again, renewed, washed, sanctified, justified and made living members of Christ, these roots remain alive in the bottom of our hearts; and, like the leprosy in the walls of the house, we never get rid of them until the earthly house of this tabernacle is dissolved.

Sin, no doubt, in the believer's heart, has no longer dominion. It is checked, controlled, mortified and crucified by *the expulsive power of the new principle of grace*. The life of a believer is a life of victory, and not of failure. But the very struggles which go on within his bosom, the fight that he finds it needful to fight daily, the watchful jealousy which he is obliged to exercise over his inner man, the contest between the flesh and the spirit, the inward 'groanings' which no one knows but he who has experienced them – all, all testify to the same great truth; all show the enormous *power* and *vitality* of sin. Mighty indeed must that foe be who, even when crucified, is still alive! Happy is that believer who understands it and, while he rejoices in Christ Jesus, has no confidence in the flesh, and while he says, 'Thanks be unto God who gives us the victory,' never forgets to watch and pray lest he fall into temptation.

4. Concerning the *guilt, vileness* and *offensiveness* of sin in the sight of God, my words will be few. I say 'few' advisedly. I do not think, in the nature of things, that mortal man can at all realize the *exceeding sinfulness of sin* in the sight of that holy and perfect One with whom we have to do. On the one hand, God is that eternal Being who charges His *angels* with error, and in whose sight the very 'heavens are not pure'. He is One who reads *thoughts* and *motives* as well as *actions* – and requires 'truth in the inward parts' (see Job 4:18; 15:15; Ps. 51:6, KJV).

We, on the other hand – poor blind creatures, here today and gone tomorrow, born in sin, surrounded by sinners, living in a constant atmosphere of weakness, infirmity and imperfection – can form none but the most inadequate conceptions of the hideousness of sin. We have no line to fathom it, and no measure by which to gauge it. The blind man can see no difference between a masterpiece of Raphael and a child's scribbling. The deaf man cannot distinguish between a penny whistle and a cathedral organ. The very animals whose smell is most offensive to us have no idea that they are offensive, and are not offensive to one another.

Fallen men and women, I believe, can have no just idea what a vile thing sin is in the sight of that God whose handiwork is absolutely perfect – perfect whether we look through telescope or microscope; perfect in the formation of a mighty planet like Jupiter, with its satellites, keeping time to a second as it rolls round the sun;

perfect in the formation of the smallest insect that crawls over a foot of ground. But let us nevertheless settle it firmly in our minds ...

that sin is the 'detestable thing that I [God] hate!';

that God's 'eyes are too pure to look on evil; you cannot tolerate wrongdoing';

that the least transgression of God's law makes us 'guilty of breaking all of it';

that the 'one who sins is the one who will die';

that 'the wages of sin is death';

that God will judge 'people's secrets';

that there is a worm that never dies and a fire that is not quenched;

that the 'wicked go down to the realm of the dead' and 'will go away to eternal punishment';

and that nothing 'impure will ever enter' heaven (Jer. 44:4; Hab. 1:13; Jas. 2:10; Ezek. 18:4; Rom. 6:23; Rom. 2:16; see Mark 9:48; Ps. 9:17; Matt. 25:46; Rev. 21:27).

These are indeed tremendous words, when we consider that they are written in the book of a most merciful God!

No proof of the *exceeding sinfulness of sin*, after all, is so overwhelming and unanswerable as the *sufferings* and *cross* of our Lord Jesus Christ, and the whole doctrine of His substitution and atonement. Terribly black must that guilt be, for which nothing but the blood of the Son of God could make satisfaction. Heavy must that weight of human sin be, which made Jesus groan and sweat drops of blood in agony at Gethsemane and cry at Golgotha, 'My God, my God, why have you forsaken me?' (Matt. 27:46).

Nothing, I am convinced, will astonish us so much, when we awake in the resurrection day, as the view we will have of *sin*, and the retrospect we will take of our own countless shortcomings and defects. Never until the hour when Christ comes the second time will we fully realize the 'sinfulness of sin'. Well might George Whitefield say, 'The anthem in heaven will be: What has God wrought!'

5. One point only remains to be considered on the subject of sin, which I dare not pass over. That point is **sin's *deceitfulness***. It is a point of most serious importance, and I venture to think it does not receive the attention which it deserves. You may see this deceitfulness in the astonishing proneness of men to regard sin as less sinful and dangerous than it is in the sight of God, and in their readiness to *extenuate* it, make *excuses* for it, and *minimize* its guilt. 'It is but a *little* one! God is merciful. God is not extreme to mark what is done amiss. We mean well. One cannot be so particular! Where is the mighty harm? We only do as others!'

Who is not familiar with this kind of language? You may see it in the long string of smooth words and phrases which men have coined in order to designate things which God calls downright wicked and ruinous to the soul. What do such expressions as 'fast', 'mirthful', 'wild', 'unsteady', 'thoughtless', 'loose' mean? They show that men try to cheat themselves into the belief that *sin is not quite as sinful as God says it is* and that they are not as bad as they really are.

You may see it in the tendency even of believers to indulge their children in questionable practices, and to blind their own eyes to the inevitable result of the love of money, of tampering with temptation, and sanctioning a low standard of family religion. I fear we do not sufficiently realize the extreme subtlety of our soul's disease. We are too apt to forget that temptation to sin will rarely present itself to us in its true colours, saying, 'I am your deadly enemy, and I want to ruin you forever in hell!' Oh, no! Sin comes to us, like Judas, with a kiss; and like Joab, with an outstretched hand and flattering words.

The forbidden fruit seemed good and desirable to Eve, yet it cast her out of Eden. The walking idly on his palace roof seemed harmless enough to David, yet it ended in adultery and murder. Sin rarely seems sin at its first beginnings. Let us then watch and pray, lest we fall into temptation. We may give wickedness smooth names, but we cannot alter its *nature* and *character* in the sight of God. Let us remember Paul's words: '... encourage one another daily ... so that none of you may be hardened by *sin's deceitfulness*' (Heb. 3:13, italics mine). It is a wise prayer in our Litany: 'from all the deceits of the world, the flesh, and the devil, Good Lord, deliver us.'

And now, before I go further, let me briefly mention two thoughts which appear to me to rise with irresistible force out of the subject.

On the one hand, I ask my readers to observe what *deep reasons we all have for humiliation and self-abasement*. Let us sit down before the picture of sin displayed to us in the Bible and consider what guilty, vile, corrupt creatures we all are in the sight of God. What need we all have of that entire change of heart called regeneration, new birth or conversion. What a mass of infirmity and imperfection cleaves to the very best of us – at our very best! What a solemn thought it is that without holiness no man shall see the Lord (Heb. 12:14). What cause we have to cry with the tax collector every night in our lives when we think of our sins of omission as well as commission, 'God, have mercy on me, a sinner' (Luke 18:13). How admirably suited are the general and communion confessions of the Prayer Book to the actual condition of all professing Christians!

How well that language suits God's children which the Prayer Book puts in the mouth of every churchman before he goes up to the communion table: 'The remembrance of our misdoings is grievous unto us; the burden is intolerable. Have mercy upon us, have mercy upon us, most merciful Father; for Your Son our Lord Jesus Christ's sake, forgive us all that is past.' How true it is that the *holiest saint* is in himself a *miserable sinner, and a debtor to mercy and grace* to the last moment of his existence.

With my whole heart I subscribe to that passage in Hooker's sermon on 'Justification', which begins:

> Let the holiest and best things we do be considered. We are never better affected unto God than when we pray; yet when we pray, how are our affections many times distracted! How little reverence do we show unto the grand majesty of God unto whom we speak! How little remorse of our own miseries! How little taste of the sweet influence of His tender mercies do we feel! Are we not as unwilling many times to begin, and as glad to make an end, as if in saying, 'Call upon Me,' He had set us a very burdensome task? It may seem somewhat extreme, which I will speak; therefore, let every one judge of it, even as his own heart shall tell him, and not otherwise; I will but only make a demand! If God should yield unto us, not as unto Abraham – if fifty, forty, thirty, twenty, yes, or if ten good people could be found in a city, for their sakes this city should not be destroyed, and if He should make us an offer thus large: 'Search all the generations of men since the Fall of our father Adam, find *one man* that has done one action which has passed from him pure, without any stain or blemish at

all, and for that one man's action only, neither man nor angel should feel the torments which are prepared for both,' do you think that this ransom to deliver men and angels could be found to be among the sons of men? The *best* things which we do have somewhat in them to be pardoned!

I am persuaded that the more light we have, the more we see our own sinfulness; the nearer we get to heaven, the more we are clothed with humility. In every age of the church you will find it true, if you will study biographies, that the most *eminent* saints – men like Bradford, Rutherford and M'Cheyne – have always been the *humblest* men.

On the other hand, I ask my readers to observe how deeply thankful we ought to be for the glorious gospel of the grace of God. There is a remedy revealed for man's need – as wide and broad and deep as man's disease! We need not be afraid to look at sin and study its nature, origin, power, extent and vileness, if we only look at the same time at the almighty medicine provided for us in the salvation that is in Jesus Christ. Though *sin* has abounded, *grace* has much more abounded ...

in the everlasting covenant of redemption, to which Father, Son and Holy Spirit are parties;

in the Mediator of that covenant, Jesus Christ, the righteous, perfect God and perfect Man in one Person;

in the *work* that He did by dying for our sins and rising again for our justification;

in the *offices* that He fills as our Priest, Substitute, Physician, Shepherd and Advocate;

in the *precious blood* He shed which can cleanse from all sin;

in the *everlasting righteousness* that He brought in;

in the *perpetual intercession* that He carries on as our Representative at God's right hand;

in His power to save to the uttermost the chief of sinners, His willingness to receive and pardon the vilest, His readiness to bear with the weakest;

in the grace of the Holy Spirit which He plants in the hearts of all His people, renewing, sanctifying and causing old things to pass away and all things to become new – in all this (and oh, what a brief sketch it is!), in all this, I say, there is a full, perfect and complete *medicine for the hideous disease of sin!* No wonder that old Flavel ends many a chapter of his admirable *Fountain of Life* (1671) with the touching words: 'Blessed be God for Jesus Christ!'

In bringing this mighty subject to a close, I feel that I have only touched the surface of it. It is one which cannot be thoroughly handled in a message like this. He who would see it treated fully and exhaustively, must turn to such masters of experimental theology as Owen and Burgess and Manton and Charnock and the other giants of the Puritan school. On subjects like this, there are no writers to be compared to the Puritans.

It only remains for me to point out some *practical uses* to which the whole doctrine of sin may be profitably turned in the present day.

a) I say, then, in the first place, that a scriptural view of sin is one of the best antidotes to that vague, dim, misty, hazy kind of theology which is so painfully current in the present age. It is vain to shut our eyes to the fact that there is a vast quantity of so-called Christianity nowadays, which you cannot declare positively unsound, but which, nevertheless, is not full measure, good weight and sixteen ounces to the pound. It is a Christianity in which there is undeniably 'something about *Christ*, and something about *grace*, and something about *faith*, and something about *repentance*, and something about *holiness*' but it is not the real 'thing as it is' in the Bible. Things are out of place and out of proportion. As old Latimer would have said, it is a kind of 'mingle-mangle', and does no good. It neither ...

exercises influence on daily conduct,

nor comforts in life,

nor gives peace in death.

And those who hold it often awake too late to find that they have got nothing solid under their feet.

Now I believe the likeliest way to cure and mend this *defective kind of religion* is to bring forward more prominently the old scriptural truth about the *sinfulness of sin*. People will never set their faces decidedly towards heaven and live like pilgrims until they really feel that they are in danger of hell. Let us all try to revive the old teaching about sin in nurseries, in schools, in training colleges, in universities.

Let us not forget that 'the law is good if one uses it properly' and that 'through the law we become conscious of our sin' (1 Tim. 1:8; Rom. 3:20; see Rom. 7:7). Let us bring the *law* to the front and press it on men's attention. Let us expound and beat out the Ten Commandments and show the length and breadth and depth and height of their requirements. This is the way of our Lord in the Sermon on the Mount. We cannot do better than follow His plan. We may depend upon it, men will never *come* to Jesus, and *stay* with Jesus, and *live* for Jesus unless they really know *why* they are to come, and what is their *need*. Those whom the Spirit draws to Jesus are those whom the Spirit has convinced of sin. Without thorough conviction of sin, men may seem to come to Jesus and follow Him for a season; but they will soon fall away and return to the world.

b) In the next place, a scriptural view of sin is one of the best antidotes to the extravagantly broad and liberal theology which is so much in vogue at the present time. The tendency of modern thought is to reject dogmas, creeds and every kind of bounds in religion. It is thought grand and wise to condemn no opinion whatever, and to pronounce all earnest and clever teachers to be trustworthy, however varied and mutually destructive their opinions may be. Everything is true – and nothing is false! Everybody is right – and nobody is wrong! Everybody is likely to be saved – and nobody is to be lost!

The atonement and substitution of Christ, the personality of the devil, the miraculous element in Scripture, the reality and eternity of future punishment – all these mighty foundation stones are coolly tossed overboard, like lumber, in order to lighten the ship of Christianity and enable it to keep pace with modern science.

If you stand up for these great Bible verities you are called narrow, illiberal, old-fashioned and a theological fossil! If you quote a Bible text you are told that all truth is not confined to the pages of an ancient Jewish book, and that free inquiry has found out many things since the book was completed!

Now, I know nothing so likely to counteract this modern plague as constant clear statements about the nature, reality, vileness, power and guilt of sin. We must charge home into the consciences of these men of broad views, and demand a plain answer to some plain questions. We must ask them to lay their hands on their hearts and tell us whether their favourite opinions comfort them in the day of sickness, in the hour of death, by the bedside of dying parents, by the grave of a beloved wife or child. We must ask them whether a vague earnestness, without definite doctrine, gives them peace at seasons like these. We must challenge them to tell us whether they do not sometimes feel a gnawing 'something' within, which all the philosophy and science in the world cannot satisfy. And then we must tell them that this gnawing 'something' is the sense of sin, guilt and corruption, which they are leaving out in their calculations. And, above all, we must tell them that nothing will ever make them feel rest, but submission to the old doctrines ...

of man's ruin, and

Christ's redemption, and

simple childlike faith in Jesus!

c) Furthermore, a right view of sin works as an antidote to a ceremonial and formal kind of Christianity, which has carried away so many in its wake. Unenlightened minds may find such a view of religion attractive in a certain sense – yet I cannot see how a ceremonial and formal religion can thoroughly satisfy the Christian. A little child is easily quieted and amused with playthings, toys and dolls – as long as he isn't hungry. Let him feel the cravings of nature within, and you will discover quickly that only food can nourish him and satisfy his hunger. Likewise, a man's soul will not find satisfaction in music and flowers and candles and incense and banners and processions and beautiful vestments and confessionals and humanly contrived ceremonies. He may amuse himself with such, but let his soul awaken and rise from the dead, and he will not rest content with these things. They will seem to him mere solemn triflings and a waste of time.

Let him see the scope of his sin – and he will also see his need for his Saviour. He hungers and thirsts – and nothing will satisfy him but the bread of life. The prominence of this form of formal and ceremonial Christianity, I dare to say, would not exist if Christians were taught more fully the nature, vileness and sinfulness of sin.

d) A right view of sin is one of the best antidotes to the overstrained theories of perfection of which we hear so much in these times. If those who press on us perfection mean nothing more than an all-round consistency and a careful attention to all the graces which make up the Christian character, reason would that we should not only bear with them but agree with them entirely. By all means, let us aim high. But if men really mean to tell us that here in this world a believer can attain to *entire* freedom from sin, live for years in unbroken and uninterrupted communion with God, and feel for months together not so much as one evil thought – I must honestly say that such an opinion appears to me very unscriptural. I go even further. I say that the opinion is very dangerous to him that holds it, and very likely to depress, discourage and keep back inquirers after salvation. I cannot find the slightest warrant in God's Word for expecting such perfection as this, while we are in the body.

I believe the words of our fifteenth Article are strictly true: that Christ alone is without sin. And that all we, though born again in Christ, 'offend in many things; and if we say we have no sin, we deceive ourselves, and the truth is not in us'. To use the language of our first homily, 'There are imperfections in our best works! We do not *love* God as much as we are bound to do, with all our heart, mind and power. We do not *fear* God as much as we ought to do. We do not *pray* to God, but with many and great imperfections. We give, forgive, believe, live and hope *imperfectly*. We speak, think and work imperfectly. We fight against the devil, the world and the flesh imperfectly. Let us, therefore, not be ashamed to confess plainly our state of imperfection.'

Once more I repeat what I have said: the best preservative against this temporary delusion about perfection which clouds some minds is a clear, full, distinct understanding of the nature, sinfulness and deceitfulness of sin!

e) In the last place, a scriptural view of sin will prove an admirable antidote to the low views of personal holiness, which are so painfully prevalent in these last days of the church. This is a very painful and delicate subject, I know – but I dare not turn away from it. It has long been my sorrowful conviction that the standard of holy living among professing Christians in this country has been gradually falling. I am afraid that Christ-like charity, kindness, good temper, unselfishness, meekness, gentleness, good nature, self-denial, zeal to do good and separation from the world are far less appreciated than they ought to be, and than they used to be in the days of our fathers.

Into the causes of this state of things, I cannot pretend to enter fully, and can only suggest conjectures for consideration. It may be that a certain profession of religion has become so fashionable and comparatively easy in the present age that the streams which were once narrow and deep have become wide and shallow; and what we have gained in outward show we have lost in quality. It may be that our contemporary affluence and comfortable lifestyles have insensibly introduced a plague of worldliness and self-indulgence and a love of ease. What were once called luxuries are now comforts and necessities, and self-denial and 'enduring hardness' are consequently little known.

It may be that the enormous amount of controversy which marks this age has insensibly dried up our spiritual life. We have too often been content with zeal for orthodoxy, and have neglected the sober realities of *daily practical godliness*.

Be the causes what they may, I must declare my own belief that the result remains. There has been of late years a lower standard of personal holiness among believers than there used to be in the days of our fathers. The whole result is that the Spirit is grieved and the matter calls for much humiliation and searching of heart.

As to the best remedy for the state of things I have mentioned, I will venture to give an opinion. I am convinced that the cure is to be found in a clearer apprehension of the nature and sinfulness of sin. We need not go back to Egypt and borrow semi-Roman 'Catholic' practices in order to revive our spiritual life. We need not restore the confessional, or return to monasticism or asceticism. Nothing of the kind! We must simply repent and do our first works. We must return to first principles. We must go back to 'the old paths'. We must sit down humbly in the presence of God, look the whole subject in the face, examine clearly what the Lord Jesus calls sin, and what the Lord Jesus calls *doing His will*. We must then try to realize that it is quite easy to live a careless, comfortable, half-worldly life, and yet at the same time to maintain evangelical principles and call ourselves Christians.

Once we see that sin is far viler and far nearer to us, and sticks more closely to us than we supposed, we will be led, I trust and believe, to get nearer to Christ. Once drawn nearer to Christ, we will drink more deeply out of His fullness and learn more thoroughly to 'live the life of faith' in Him, as Paul did. Once taught to live the life of faith in Jesus, and abiding in Him, we will bear more fruit, will find ourselves more strong for duty, more patient in trial, more watchful over our poor weak hearts, and more like our Master in all our little daily ways.

Just in proportion as we realize how much Christ has done for us, will we labour to do much for Christ. Much forgiven, we will love much. In short, as the apostle says, 'we all, who with unveiled faces contemplate the Lord's glory, are being transformed into his image ... which comes from the Lord, who is the Spirit' (2 Cor. 3:18).

Whatever some may please to think or say, there can be no doubt that an increased feeling about holiness is one of the signs of the times. Conferences for the promotion of 'spiritual life' are becoming common in the present day. The subject of 'spiritual life' finds a place on platforms almost every year. It has awakened an amount of interest and general attention throughout the land, for which we ought to be thankful. Any movement, based on sound principles, which helps to deepen our spiritual life and increase our personal holiness, will be a real blessing to the Church of England. It will do much to draw us together and heal our unhappy divisions. It may bring down some fresh outpouring of the grace of the Spirit and be 'life from the dead' in these later times. But sure I am, as I said in the beginning, we must begin low if we would build high. I am convinced that *the first step towards attaining a higher standard of holiness is to realize more fully the amazing sinfulness of sin!*

2

Sanctification

'Sanctify them by the truth'

(John 17:17)

*'It is God's will that you
should be sanctified'*

(1 Thess. 4:3)

The subject of sanctification is one which many, I fear, dislike exceedingly. Some even turn from it with scorn and disdain. The very last thing they would like is to be a 'saint' or a 'sanctified' man. Yet the subject does not deserve to be treated in this way. It is not an enemy – but a friend.

It is a subject of the utmost importance to our souls. If the Bible is true, it is certain that unless we are 'sanctified' we shall not be saved. There are three things which, according to the Bible, are absolutely necessary to the salvation of every man and woman in Christendom.

These three are ...

justification,

regeneration and

sanctification.

All three meet in every child of God – he is born again, and justified, and sanctified. He who lacks any one of these three things is not a true Christian in the sight of God and, dying in that condition, will not be found in heaven and glorified in the last day.

It is a subject which is peculiarly seasonable in the present day. Strange doctrines have risen up of late upon the whole subject of sanctification. Some appear to confound it with justification. Others fritter it away to nothing, under the presence of zeal for free grace, and practically neglect it altogether. Others are so much afraid of 'works' being made a part of justification that they can hardly find any place at all for 'works' in their religion. Others set up a wrong standard of sanctification before their eyes and, failing to attain it, waste their lives in repeated moves from church to church, chapel to chapel and sect to sect in the vain hope that they will find what they want. In a day like this, a calm examination of the subject, as a great leading doctrine of the gospel, may be of great use to our souls.

Now let us consider ...

the true *nature* of sanctification,

its visible *marks*, and

how it is *compared* to and *contrasted* with justification.

If, unhappily, the reader is one of those who cares for nothing but this world, and makes no profession of religion, I cannot expect him to take much interest in what I am writing. You will probably think it an affair of 'words and names' and nice questions, about which it matters nothing what you hold and believe. But if you are a thoughtful, reasonable, sensible Christian, I venture to say that you will find it worthwhile to have some clear ideas about sanctification.

The nature of sanctification

Sanctification is that inward spiritual work which the Lord Jesus Christ works in a man by the Holy Spirit, when He calls him to be a true believer. He not only *washes* him from his sins in His own blood, but He also ...

separates him from his natural love of sin and the world,

puts a *new principle* in his heart, and

makes him *practically godly* in life.

The instrument by which the Spirit effects this work is generally the Word of God, though He sometimes uses afflictions and providential visitations 'without the word' (1 Pet. 3:1, KJV). The subject of this work of Christ by His Spirit is called in Scripture a 'sanctified' man.

He who supposes that Jesus Christ only lived and died and rose again in order to provide justification and forgiveness of sins for His people has yet much to learn. Whether he knows it or not, he is dishonouring our blessed Lord and making Him only a half Saviour. The Lord Jesus has undertaken everything that His people's souls require: not only to deliver them from the *guilt* of their sins, by His atoning death, but from the *dominion* of their sins, by placing in their hearts the Holy Spirit; not only to *justify* them but also to *sanctify* them. He is, thus, not only their 'righteousness' but their 'sanctification' (1 Cor. 1:30, KJV).

Let us hear what the Bible says: 'For them I sanctify myself, that they too may be truly sanctified'; 'Christ loved the church and gave himself up for her to make her holy, cleansing her'; Christ 'gave himself for us to redeem us from all wickedness and to purify for himself a people that are his very own, eager to do what is good'; Christ '" ... bore our sins" in his body on the cross, so that we might die to sins and live for righteousness'; God has now 'reconciled you by Christ's physical body through death to present you holy in his sight, without blemish and free from accusation' (John 17:19; Eph. 5:25,26; Titus 2:14; 1 Pet. 2:24; Col. 1:22).

Let the meaning of these five texts be carefully considered. If words mean anything, they teach that Christ undertakes the *sanctification* no less than the *justification* of His believing people. Both are alike provided for in that 'everlasting covenant, arranged and secured in every part' (2 Sam. 23:5), of which the Mediator is Christ. In fact, Christ in one place is called He 'who makes people holy', and His people 'those who are made holy' (Heb. 2:11).

The subject before us is of such deep and vast importance that it requires fencing, guarding, clearing up and marking out on every side. A doctrine which is needful to salvation can never be too sharply developed or brought too fully into light. To clear away the confusion between doctrines and doctrines, which is so unhappily common among Christians, and to map out the precise relation between truths and truths in religion, is one way to attain accuracy in our theology.

I shall therefore not hesitate to lay before my readers a series of connected propositions or statements, drawn from Scripture, which I think will be found useful in defining the exact nature of sanctification. Each proposition would admit of being expanded and handled more fully, and all of them deserve private thought and consideration. Some of them may be disputed and contradicted; but I doubt whether any of them can be overthrown or proved untrue. I only ask for them a fair and impartial hearing.

1. Sanctification is the invariable result of that vital union with Christ which true faith gives to a Christian. 'If you remain in me and I in you, you will bear much fruit' (John 15:5). The branch which bears no fruit is no living branch of the vine. The union with Christ which produces no effect on heart and life is a mere formal union, which is worthless before God. The faith which has not a sanctifying influence on the character is no better than the faith of devils. It is a 'dead faith, because it is alone'. It is not the gift of God. It is not the faith of God's elect. In short, where there is no sanctification of life, there is no real faith in Christ.

True faith works by love. It constrains a man to live unto the Lord from a deep sense of gratitude for redemption. It makes him feel that he can never do too much for Him who died for him. Being much forgiven he loves much. He whom the blood cleanses walks in the light. He who has real living hope in Christ purifies himself even as He is pure (Jas. 2:17–20; Titus 1:1; Gal. 5:6; 1 John 1:7; 3:3).

2. Sanctification is the outcome and inseparable consequence of regeneration. He who is born again and made a new creature receives a new nature and a new principle and always lives a new life. A regeneration, which a man can have and yet live carelessly in sin or worldliness, is a regeneration invented by uninspired theologians but never mentioned in Scripture. On the contrary, John expressly says that he who is born of God ...

'does what is right',

does not 'continue to sin',

'love[s] each other' (their brothers and sisters in Christ), and

'overcomes the world', and

that Jesus 'keeps them safe'

(1 John 2:29; 3:9–14; 5:4–18).

Simply put, the lack of sanctification is a sign of non-regeneration. Where there is no holy *life*, there has been no holy *birth*. This is a hard saying – but a biblical truth; whomever is born of God, it is written, 'cannot go on sinning, because they have been born of God' (1 John 3:9).

3. Sanctification is the only certain evidence of that indwelling of the Holy Spirit which is essential to salvation. '... if anyone does not have the Spirit of Christ, they do not belong to Christ' (Rom. 8:9). The Spirit never lies dormant and idle within the soul. He always makes His presence known by the fruit He causes to be borne in heart, character and life. '... the fruit of the Spirit,' says Paul, 'is love, joy, peace, forbearance, kindness, goodness, faithfulness, gentleness and self-control' (Gal. 5:22,23). Where these things are to be found, there is the Spirit; where these things are lacking, men are dead before God.

The Spirit is compared to the wind; and, like the wind, He cannot be seen by our bodily eyes. But, just as we know there is a wind by the *effect* it produces on waves and trees and smoke, so we may know the Spirit is in a man by the effects He produces in the man's conduct. It is nonsense to suppose that we have the Spirit if we do not also 'keep in step with the Spirit' (Gal. 5:25).

We may depend on it as a positive certainty that where there is no holy living, there is no Holy Spirit! The *seal* that the Spirit stamps on Christ's people is *sanctification*. As many as are actually 'led by the Spirit of God', they and they only 'are the children of God' (Rom. 8:14).

4. Sanctification is the only sure mark of God's election. The names and number of the elect are a secret thing, no doubt, which God has wisely kept in His own power and not revealed to man. It is not given to us in this world to study the pages of the book of life and see if our names are there. But if there is one thing clearly and plainly laid down about election, it is this – that *elect men and women may be known and distinguished by holy lives*. It is expressly written that they are 'elect ... through the sanctifying work of the Spirit', 'God chose [them] ... to be saved through the sanctifying work of the Sprit' and 'predestined [them] to be conformed to the image of his Son', and God 'chose [them] ... before the creation of the world to be holy'. Hence, when Paul saw the working 'faith' and labouring 'love' and patient 'hope' of the Thessalonian believers, he said, I know 'your election of God' (1 Pet. 1:1,2; 2 Thess. 2:13; Rom. 8:29; Eph. 1:4; 1 Thess. 1:3,4, KJV).

He who boasts of being one of God's elect, while he is wilfully and habitually living in sin, is only deceiving himself and talking wicked blasphemy. Of course, it is hard to know exactly *what* people really are; and many who make a fair show outwardly in religion may turn out at last to be rotten-hearted hypocrites. But where there is not, at least, some appearance of sanctification, we may be quite certain there is no election. The church catechism correctly and wisely teaches that the Holy Spirit 'sanctifies ... all the elect people of God'.

5. Sanctification is a reality that will always be *seen*. Like the great Head of the church, from whom it springs, it cannot be hidden. 'Each tree is recognised by its own *fruit*' (Luke 6:44, italics mine). A truly sanctified person may be so clothed with humility that he can see in himself nothing but infirmity and defects. Like Moses, when he came down from the mount, he may not be conscious that his face shines. Like the righteous, in the mighty parable of the sheep and the goats, he may not see that he has done anything worthy of his Master's notice and commendation: 'Then the righteous will answer him, "Lord, when did we see you hungry and feed you, or thirsty and give you something to drink?"' (Matt. 25:37). But whether he sees it himself or not, others will always see in him a tone and taste and character and habit of life unlike that of other men.

The very idea of a man being 'sanctified' while no holiness can be seen in his life is flat nonsense and a misuse of words. *Light* may be very dim; but if there is only a spark in a dark room, it will be seen. *Life* may be very feeble; but if the pulse only beats a little, it will be felt. It is just the same with a sanctified man; his sanctification will be something felt and seen, though he himself may not understand it. *A 'saint' in whom nothing can be seen but worldliness or sin is a kind of monster not recognized in the Bible!*

6. Sanctification is a reality for which every believer is responsible. In saying this, I would not be mistaken. I hold as strongly as anyone that every man on earth is accountable to God, and that all the lost will be speechless and without excuse at the last day. Every man has power to 'forfeit their soul' (Matt. 16:26). But, while I hold this, I maintain that believers are eminently and peculiarly responsible, and under a special obligation to live holy lives. They are not as others, dead and blind and unrenewed; they are alive unto God and have light and knowledge and a new principle within them. Whose fault is it, if they are not holy – but their own? On whom can they throw the blame, if they are not sanctified – but themselves? God, who has given them grace and a new heart and a new nature, has deprived them of all excuse if they do not live for His praise.

This is a point which is far too much forgotten. A man who professes to be a true Christian, while he sits still, content with a very low degree of sanctification (if indeed he has any at all), and coolly tells you he 'can do nothing' is a very pitiable sight, and a very ignorant man! Against this delusion, let us watch and be on our guard. The Word of God always addresses its precepts to believers as accountable and responsible beings. If the Saviour of sinners gives us renewing grace and calls us by His Spirit, we may be sure that He expects us to use our grace and not to go to sleep. It is forgetfulness of this which causes many believers to 'grieve the Holy Spirit' (Eph. 4:30) and makes them very useless and uncomfortable Christians.

7. Sanctification is a thing which admits of growth and degrees. A man may climb from one step to another in holiness, and be far more sanctified at one period of his life than another. More *pardoned* and more *justified* than he is when he first believes he cannot be, though he may feel it more. More *sanctified* he certainly may be – because every grace in his new character may be strengthened, enlarged and deepened. This is the evident meaning of our Lord's last prayer for His disciples when He used the words, 'Sanctify them', and of Paul's prayer for the Thessalonians: 'God himself, the God of peace, sanctify you' (John 17:17; 1 Thess. 5:23). In both cases, the expression plainly implies the possibility of increased sanctification, while such an expression as 'justify them' is never once in Scripture applied to a believer, because he cannot be more justified than he is.

I can find no warrant in Scripture for the doctrine of 'imputed sanctification'. It is a doctrine which confuses things that differ and leads to very evil consequences. Not least, it is a doctrine which is flatly contradicted by the experience of all the most eminent Christians. If there is any point on which God's holiest saints agree, it is this: that they *see* more, and *know* more, and *feel* more, and *do* more, and *repent* more, and *believe* more as they get on in spiritual life, and in proportion to the closeness of their walk with God. In short, they 'grow in the grace' as Peter exhorts believers to do, and 'do this more and more', according to the words of Paul (2 Pet. 3:18; 1 Thess. 4:1).

8. Sanctification depends greatly on a diligent use of scriptural means. The 'means of grace' are such as Bible-reading, private prayer and regularly worshipping God in church, wherein one hears the Word taught and participates in the Lord's Supper. I lay it down as a simple matter of fact that no one who is careless about such things must ever expect to make much progress in sanctification. I can find no record of any eminent saint who ever neglected them.

They are appointed channels through which the Holy Spirit conveys fresh supplies of grace to the soul, and strengthens the work which He has begun in the inward man. Let men call this *legal doctrine* if they please, but I will never shrink from declaring my belief that there are no 'spiritual gains without pains'. Our God is a God who works by *means*, and He will never bless the soul of that man who pretends to be so high and spiritual that he can get on without them.

9. Sanctification is a thing which does not prevent a man having a great deal of inward spiritual conflict. By conflict I mean a struggle within the heart between the old nature and the new, the flesh and the spirit, which are to be found together in every believer (Gal. 5:17). A deep sense of that struggle, and a vast amount of mental discomfort from it, are no proof that a man is not sanctified. No, rather, I believe, they are symptoms of our healthy spiritual condition, and prove that we are not dead, but alive. A true Christian is one who has not only *peace* of conscience but *war* within. He may be known by his *warfare* as well as by his *peace*.

In saying this, I do not forget that I am contradicting the views of some well-meaning Christians who hold the doctrine called 'sinless perfection'. I cannot help that. I believe that what I say is confirmed by the language of Paul in the seventh chapter of Romans. That chapter I commend to the careful study of all my readers. I am quite satisfied that it does not describe the experience of an unconverted man, or of a young and unestablished Christian, but of an old experienced saint in close communion with God. None but such a man could say, 'in my inner being I delight in God's law' (Rom. 7:22).

I believe, furthermore, that what I say is proved by the experience of all the most eminent servants of Christ that have ever lived. The full proof is to be seen in their journals, their autobiographies and their lives.

Believing all this, I shall never hesitate to tell people that inward conflict is no proof that a man is not holy, and that they must not think they are not sanctified because they do not feel entirely free from inward struggle. Such freedom from conflict we shall doubtless have in heaven, but we shall never enjoy it in this present world. The heart of the best Christian, even at his best, is a field occupied by two rival camps, and the 'company of two armies' (Song 6:13, KJV). Let the words of the thirteenth and fifteenth Articles be well considered: 'The infection of nature remains in those who are regenerated ... although baptized and born again in Christ, yet [we] offend in many things; and if we say we have no sin, we deceive ourselves, and the truth is not in us' (fifteenth Article).

10. Sanctification is a thing which cannot *justify* a man, and yet it *pleases God*. The holiest actions of the holiest saint that ever lived are all more or less full of defects and imperfections. They are either wrong in their motive, or defective in their performance, and in themselves are nothing better than 'splendid sins' deserving God's wrath and condemnation. To suppose that such actions can stand the severity of God's judgement, atone for sin, and merit heaven is simply absurd. '... no one will be declared righteous in God's sight by the works of the law ... we maintain that a person is justified by faith apart from the works of the law' (Rom. 3:20–28).

The only righteousness in which we can appear before God is the righteousness of another, even the perfect righteousness of our Substitute and Representative, Jesus Christ the Lord. His work and not our work is our only title to heaven. This is a truth which we should be ready to die to maintain.

For all this, however, the Bible distinctly teaches that the holy actions of a sanctified man, although imperfect, are pleasing in the sight of God. '... with such sacrifices God is pleased' (Heb. 13:16); '... obey your parents ... for this pleases the Lord' (Col. 3:20); '... we keep his commands and do what pleases him' (1 John 3:22). Let this never be forgotten, for it is a very comforting doctrine.

Just as a parent is pleased with the efforts of his little child to please him, though it be only by picking a daisy, or walking across a room, so is our Father in heaven pleased with the poor performances of His believing children. He looks at the *motive, principle* and *intention* of their actions, and not merely at their quantity and quality. He regards them as members of His own dear Son, and for His sake, wherever there is a single eye, He is well pleased.

11. Sanctification is a thing which will be found absolutely necessary as a witness to our character, in the great day of judgement. It will be utterly useless to plead that we believed in Christ unless our faith has had some sanctifying effect and been seen in our lives. Evidence, evidence, evidence will be the one thing needed when the great white throne is set, when the books are opened, when the graves give up their tenants, when the dead are arraigned before the bar of God. Without some evidence that our faith in Christ was real and genuine, we shall only rise again to be condemned. I can find no evidence that will be admitted in that day, except sanctification. The question will not be how we *talked* and what we *professed*, but how we *lived* and what we *did*.

Let no man deceive himself on this point. If anything is certain about the future, it is certain that there will be a judgement; and if anything is certain about judgement, it is certain that men's 'works' and 'doings' will be considered and examined in it (John 5:29; 2 Cor. 5:10; Rev. 20:13). He who supposes works are of no importance because they cannot justify us is a very ignorant Christian. Unless he opens his eyes, he will find to his cost that if he comes to the bar of God without some evidence of grace, he had better never have been born.

12. Sanctification, in the last place, is absolutely necessary in order to train and prepare us for heaven. Most men hope to go to heaven when they die, but few, it may be feared, take the trouble to consider whether they would enjoy heaven if they got there. Heaven is essentially a holy place; its inhabitants are all holy; its occupations are all holy. To be really happy in heaven, it is clear and plain that we must be somewhat trained and made ready for heaven while we are on earth. The notion of a purgatory after death, which shall turn sinners into saints, is a lying invention of man, and is nowhere taught in the Bible. We must be saints before we die if we are to be saints afterwards in glory.

The favourite idea of many, that dying men need nothing except absolution and forgiveness of sins to fit them for their great change, is a profound delusion. We need the work of the Holy Spirit – as well as the work of Christ; we need renewal of the heart – as well as the atoning blood; we need to be sanctified – as well as to be justified.

It is common to hear people saying on their deathbeds, 'I only want the Lord to forgive me my sins, and take me to rest.' But those who say such things forget that the rest of heaven would be utterly useless if we had no heart to enjoy it! What could an unsanctified man do in heaven, if by any chance he got there? Let that question be fairly looked in the face and fairly answered.

No man can possibly be happy in a place where he is not in his element and where all around him is not congenial to his tastes, habits and character. When an eagle is happy in an iron cage, when a sheep is happy in the water, when an owl is happy in the blaze of noonday sun, when a fish is happy on the dry land – then, and not until then, will I admit that the unsanctified man could be happy in heaven.

The visible evidence or marks of sanctification

What are the visible marks of a sanctified man? What may we expect to see in him? This is a very wide and difficult department of our subject. It is wide because it necessitates the mention of many details which cannot be handled fully in the limits of a message like this. It is difficult because it cannot possibly be treated without giving offence. But truth should be spoken despite risk, and truth of this great magnitude should especially be spoken in our present day.

1. True sanctification then does not consist in mere talk about religion. This is a point which ought never to be forgotten. The vast increase of education and preaching in these latter days makes it absolutely necessary to raise a warning voice. People hear so much of gospel truth that they contract *an unholy familiarity* with its words and phrases, and sometimes talk so fluently about its doctrines that you might think them true Christians. In fact it is sickening and disgusting to hear the cool and flippant language which many pour out about 'conversion', 'the Saviour', 'the gospel', 'finding peace', 'free grace' and the like, while they are *notoriously serving sin or living for the world.*

Can we doubt that such talk is abominable in God's sight and is little better than cursing, swearing and taking God's name in vain? The tongue is not the only member that Christ bids us give to His service. God does not want His people to be mere empty tubs, sounding brass and tinkling cymbals. We must be sanctified, not only 'with words or speech but with actions and in truth' (1 John 3:18).

2. True sanctification does not consist in temporary religious feelings. This again is a point about which a warning is greatly needed. Mission services and revival meetings are attracting great attention in every part of the land, and producing a great sensation. The Church of England seems to have taken a new lease of life and exhibits a new activity – and we ought to thank God for it. But these things have their attendant dangers as well as their advantages. Wherever *wheat* is sown, the devil is sure to sow *tares*. Many, it may be feared, appear moved and touched and roused under the preaching of the gospel, while in reality their hearts are not changed at all. A kind of animal excitement from the contagion of seeing others weeping, rejoicing or affected is the true account of their case. Their wounds are only skin deep, and the peace they profess to feel is skin deep also.

Like the stony ground hearers, they receive the Word with joy (Matt. 13:20); but after a little while they fall away, go back to the world and are harder and worse than before! Like Jonah's gourd, they come up suddenly in a night, and they perish in a night. Let these things not be forgotten. Let us beware in this day of healing wounds slightly; and crying, 'Peace, peace,' when there is no peace. Let us urge on everyone who exhibits new interest in religion to be content with nothing short of the deep, solid, sanctifying work of the Holy Spirit.

Emotional feelings, after false religious excitement, is a most deadly disease of soul. When the devil is only temporarily cast out of a man in the heat of a revival, and by and by returns to his house, the last state becomes worse than the first. Better a thousand times to begin more slowly and then 'continue in the Word' steadfastly than begin in a hurry, without *counting the cost*, and by and by look back, with Lot's wife, and return to the world. I declare I know no state of soul more dangerous than to imagine we are born again and sanctified by the Holy Spirit, because we have picked up a few religious feelings.

3. True sanctification does not consist in outward formalism and external devoutness. This is an enormous delusion, but unhappily a very common one. Thousands appear to imagine that true holiness is to be seen in an excessive quantity of bodily religion – in constant attendance on church services, reception of the Lord's Supper and observance of fasts and saints' days; in multiplied bowings and turnings and gestures and postures during public worship; in wearing peculiar dresses, and the use of pictures and crosses.

I freely admit that some people take up these things from conscientious motives and actually believe that they help their souls.

But I am afraid that in many cases, this *external religiousness* is made a substitute for *inward holiness*, and I am quite certain that it falls utterly short of sanctification of heart. Above all, when I see that many followers of this external and formal style of Christianity are absorbed in worldliness and plunge headlong into its pomp and vanities without shame, I feel that there is need of very plain speaking on the subject. There may be an immense amount of 'bodily service' while there is not a jot of real sanctification!

4. Sanctification does not consist in retirement from our place in life, and the renunciation of our social duties. In every age it has been a snare with many, to take up this line in the pursuit of holiness. Hundreds of hermits have buried themselves in some wilderness, and thousands of men and women have shut themselves up within the walls of monasteries and convents under the vain idea that by so doing, they would escape sin and become eminently holy. They have forgotten that *no bolts and bars can keep out the devil* and that, wherever we go, we carry that root of all evil, our own hearts. To become a monk or a nun or to join a monastery or convent is not the high road to sanctification.

True holiness does not make a Christian evade difficulties but face and overcome them. Christ would have His people show that His grace is not a mere hot-house plant, which can only thrive under shelter, but a strong, hardy thing which can flourish in every relation of life. It is doing our duty, in that state to which God has called us, like *salt* in the midst of corruption and *light* in the midst of darkness, which is a primary element in sanctification.

It is not the man who hides himself in a cave, but the man who glorifies God as master or servant, parent or child, in the family and in the street, in business and in trade, who is the scriptural type of a sanctified man. Our Master Himself said in His last prayer, 'My prayer is not that you take them out of the world but that you protect them from the evil one' (John 17:15).

5. Sanctification is not merely the occasional performance of right actions. Rather, it is the continual work of a new heavenly principle within, which runs through one's daily conduct in everything he does, big or small. It is not like a pump, which only sends forth water when worked upon from without, but like a perpetual fountain, from which a stream is ever flowing spontaneously and naturally. Even Herod, when he heard John the Baptist, 'did many things' – while his heart was utterly wrong in the sight of God (Mark 6:20, KJV).

Just so, there are scores of people in the present day who seem to have spasmodic fits of 'goodness', as it is called, and do many right things under the influence of sickness, affliction, death in the family, public calamities or a sudden qualm of conscience. Yet all the time any intelligent observer can see plainly that they are not converted and that they know nothing of 'sanctification'. A true saint, like Hezekiah, will be *wholehearted*. He will count God's commandments concerning all things to be right, and 'hate every wrong path' (2 Chr. 31:21; Ps. 119:104).

6. Genuine sanctification will show itself in habitual respect to God's law, and habitual effort to live in obedience to it as the rule of life. There is no greater mistake than to suppose that a Christian has nothing to do with the law and the Ten Commandments, because he cannot be justified by keeping them. The same Holy Spirit who convinces the believer of sin by the law and leads him to Christ for justification will always lead him to a spiritual use of the law, as a friendly guide in the pursuit of sanctification. Our Lord Jesus Christ never made light of the Ten Commandments; on the contrary, in His first public discourse, the Sermon on the Mount, He expounded them and showed the searching nature of their requirements. Paul never made light of the law; on the contrary, he says, 'the law is good if one uses it properly'; '... in my inner being I delight in God's law' (1 Tim. 1:8; Rom. 7:22).

He who pretends to be a saint while he sneers at the Ten Commandments and thinks nothing of lying, hypocrisy, swindling, ill temper, slander, drunkenness and breach of the seventh commandment is under a fearful delusion. He will find it hard to prove that he is a 'saint' in the last day!

7. Genuine sanctification will show itself in a habitual endeavour to do Christ's will, and to live by His practical precepts. These precepts are to be found scattered everywhere throughout the four Gospels, and especially in the Sermon on the Mount. He who supposes they were spoken without the intention of promoting holiness, and that a Christian need not attend to them in his daily life, is really little better than a lunatic, and at any rate is a grossly ignorant person.

To hear some men talk and read some men's writings, one might imagine that our blessed Lord, when He was on earth, never taught anything but doctrine – and left practical duties to be taught by others! The slightest knowledge of the four Gospels ought to tell us that this is a complete mistake. What His disciples ought to be and to do is continually brought forward in our Lord's teaching. A truly sanctified man will never forget this. He serves a Master who said, 'You are my friends if you do what I command' (John 15:14).

8. Genuine sanctification will show itself in a habitual desire to live up to the standard which Paul sets before the churches in his writings. That standard is to be found in the closing chapters of nearly all his epistles. The common idea of many people that Paul's writings are full of nothing but doctrinal statements and controversial subjects – justification, election, predestination, prophecy and the like – is an entire delusion and a melancholy proof of the ignorance of Scripture which prevails in these latter days. I defy anyone to read Paul's writings carefully, without finding in them a large quantity of plain practical directions about the Christian's duty in every relation of life, and about our daily habits, temper and behaviour to one another. These directions were written down by inspiration of God for the perpetual guidance of professing Christians. He who does not attend to them may possibly pass muster as a member of a church or a chapel, but he certainly is not what the Bible calls a 'sanctified' man.

9. Genuine sanctification will show itself in habitual attention to the *active graces* which our Lord so beautifully exemplified, and especially to the grace of love. 'A new command I give you: love one another. As I have loved you, so you must love one another. By this everyone will know that you are my disciples, if you love one another' (John 13:34,35). A sanctified man will try to do good in the world, and to lessen the sorrow and increase the happiness of all around him. He will aim to be like his Master – full of kindness and love to everyone – and this not in word only, by calling people 'dear', but by deeds and actions and self-denying work, according as he has opportunity.

The selfish professor who wraps himself up in his own conceit of superior knowledge and seems to care nothing whether others sink or swim, go to heaven or hell, so long as he walks to church or chapel in his Sunday best and is called a 'sound member' – such a man knows nothing of sanctification. He may think himself a saint on earth, but he will not be a saint in heaven! Christ will never be found the Saviour of those who know nothing of following His example. Saving faith and real converting grace will always produce some conformity to the image of Jesus (Col. 3:10). 'For those God foreknew he also predestined to be conformed to the image of his Son' (Rom. 8:29).

10. Genuine sanctification, in the last place, will show itself in habitual attention to the *passive graces* of Christianity. When I speak of passive graces, I mean those graces which are especially shown in submission to the will of God, and in bearing and forbearing towards one another. Few people, perhaps, unless they have examined the point, have an idea how much is said about these graces in the New Testament, and how important a place they seem to fill. This is the special point which Peter dwells upon in commending our Lord Jesus Christ's example to our notice: 'To this you were called, because Christ suffered for you, leaving you an *example, that you should follow in his steps*. "He committed no sin, and no deceit was found in his mouth." When they hurled their insults at him, he did not retaliate; when he suffered, he made no threats. Instead, he entrusted himself to him who judges justly' (1 Pet. 2:21–23, italics mine).

This is the one piece of profession which the Lord's Prayer requires us to make: 'Forgive us our trespasses – *as* we forgive those who trespass against us', and the one point that is commented upon at the end of the prayer. This is the point which occupies one third of the list of the fruits of the Spirit supplied by Paul. Nine are named and three of these, forbearance, kindness and gentleness (translated as 'longsuffering', 'gentlessness' and 'meekness' in the KJV), are unquestionably *passive* graces (Gal. 5:22,23).

I must plainly say that I do not think this subject is sufficiently considered by Christians. The passive graces are no doubt harder to attain than the active ones, but they are precisely the graces which have the greatest influence on the world. Of one thing I feel very sure: it is nonsense to pretend to sanctification, unless we follow after the meekness, gentleness, patience and forgivingness of which the Bible makes so much. People who are habitually giving way to peevish and cross tempers in daily life and are constantly sharp with their tongues and disagreeable to all around them, spiteful people, vindictive people, revengeful people, malicious people – of whom, alas, the world is only too full – all such know little as they should know about sanctification.

The distinction between justification and sanctification

I now propose to consider, in the last place, the distinction between justification and sanctification. Wherein do they agree, and wherein do they differ?

This branch of our subject is one of great importance, though I fear it will not seem so to all my readers. I shall handle it briefly, but I dare not pass it over altogether. Too many are apt to look at nothing but the surface of things in religion and regard distinctions in theology as questions of 'words and names' which are of little real value. But I warn all who are in earnest about their souls that the discomfort which arises from not 'distinguishing things that differ' in Christian doctrine is very great indeed. And I especially advise them, if they love peace, to seek clear views about the matter before us.

We must always remember that justification and sanctification are two distinct things. Yet there are points in which they agree, and points in which they differ. Let us try to find out what they are.

In what, then, are justification and sanctification *alike*?

1. Both proceed originally from the free grace of God. It is of His gift alone that believers are justified or sanctified at all.

2. Both are part of that great work of salvation which Christ, in the eternal covenant, has undertaken on behalf of His people. Christ is the fountain of life, from which pardon and holiness both flow. The root of each is Christ.

3. Both are to be found in the same people. Those who are justified are always sanctified, and those who are sanctified are always justified. God has joined them together, and they cannot be put asunder.

4. Both begin at the same time. The moment a person is a justified person he also begins to be a sanctified person. He may not *feel* it, but it is a *fact*.

5. Both are alike necessary to salvation. No one ever reached heaven ...

without a renewed heart – as well as forgiveness;

without the Spirit's grace – as well as the blood of Christ;

without a fitness for eternal glory – as well as a title.

The one is just as necessary as the other.

Such are the points on which justification and sanctification agree. Let us now reverse the picture, and see wherein they *differ*.

1. Justification is the *reckoning* and counting a man to be righteous for the sake of another, even Jesus Christ the Lord.

Sanctification is the actual *making* a man inwardly righteous, though it may be in a very feeble degree.

2. The righteousness we have by our justification is not our own, but the everlasting perfect righteousness of our great Mediator Christ, imputed to us, and made our own by faith.

The righteousness we have by sanctification is our own righteousness, imparted, inherent and wrought in us by the Holy Spirit, but mingled with much infirmity and imperfection.

3. In justification our own works have no place at all, and simple faith in Christ is the one thing needful.

In sanctification our own works are of vast importance, and God bids us fight and watch and pray and strive and take pains and labour.

4. Justification is a finished and complete work, and a man is perfectly justified the moment he believes.

Sanctification is an imperfect work, comparatively, and will never be perfected until we reach heaven.

5. Justification admits of no growth or increase: a man is as much justified the hour he first comes to Christ by faith as he will be to all eternity.

Sanctification is eminently a progressive work and admits of continual growth and enlargement so long as a man lives.

6. Justification has special reference to our persons, our standing in God's sight and our deliverance from guilt.

Sanctification has special reference to our natures and the moral renewal of our hearts.

7. Justification gives us our title to heaven and boldness to enter in.

Sanctification gives us our fitness for heaven and prepares us to enjoy it when we dwell there.

8. Justification is the act of God for us and is not easily discerned by others.

Sanctification is the work of God within us and cannot be hidden in its outward manifestation from the eyes of men.

I commend these distinctions to the attention of all my readers, and I ask them to ponder them well. I am persuaded that one great cause of the darkness and uncomfortable feelings of many well-meaning people in the matter of religion is their habit of confounding, and not distinguishing, justification and sanctification.

It can never be too strongly impressed on our minds, that they are *two separate things*. Yet, *they cannot be separated* and everyone that is a partaker of *either* is a partaker of *both*. But never, never ought they to be confounded, and never ought the distinction between them to be forgotten.

Practical reflections

The nature and visible marks of sanctification have been brought before us. What practical reflections ought the whole matter to raise in our minds?

1. For one thing, let us all awake to a sense of the perilous state of many *professing* Christians. Without holiness, no man shall see the Lord; without sanctification, there is no salvation (Heb. 12:14). Then what an enormous amount of so-called religion there is, which is perfectly useless! What an immense proportion of church-goers and chapel-goers are in the broad road that leads to destruction! The thought is dreadful, crushing and overwhelming. Oh, that preachers and teachers would open their eyes and realize the condition of souls around them! Oh, that men could be persuaded to 'flee from the wrath to come'! If unsanctified souls can be saved and go to heaven, the Bible is not true. Yet the Bible is true and cannot lie. What must the end be?

2. Let us make sure work of our own condition and never rest until we feel and know that we are 'sanctified' ourselves. What are our tastes and choices and likings and inclinations? This is the great testing question. It matters little what we wish and what we hope and what we desire to be before we die. What *are* we now? What are we doing? Are we sanctified – or not? If not, the fault is all our own.

3. If we would be sanctified, our course is clear and plain: we must begin with Christ. We must go to Him as sinners, with no plea but that of utter need, and cast our souls on Him by faith – for peace and reconciliation with God. We must place ourselves in His hands, as in the hands of a good physician, and cry to Him for mercy and grace. We must wait for nothing to bring with us, as a recommendation. The very first step towards sanctification, no less than justification, is to come with faith to Christ. We must first *live* – and then *work*.

4. If we would grow in holiness and become more sanctified, we must continually go on as we began, and be ever making fresh applications to Christ. He is the Head from which every member must be supplied (Eph. 4:16). To live the life of daily faith in the Son of God, and to be daily drawing out of His fullness the promised grace and strength which He has laid up for His people – this is the grand secret of progressive sanctification. Believers who seem at a standstill are generally neglecting close communion with Jesus, and so grieving the Spirit. He who prayed, 'Sanctify them,' the last night before His crucifixion is infinitely willing to help everyone who by faith applies to Him for help, and desires to be made more holy.

51

5. Let us not expect too much from our own hearts here below. At our best, we shall find in ourselves daily cause for humiliation and discover that we are needy debtors to mercy and grace every hour. The more light we have, the more we shall see our own imperfection! Sinners we were when we began, and sinners we shall find ourselves as we go on. Renewed, pardoned, justified – yet *sinners to the very last*. Our *absolute* perfection is yet to come, and the expectation of it is one reason why we should long for heaven.

6. Finally, let us never be ashamed of making much of sanctification, and contending for a high standard of holiness. While some are satisfied with a miserably low degree of attainment, and others are not ashamed to live on without any holiness at all – content with a mere round of church-going and chapel-going but never getting on, like a horse in a mill – let us stand fast in the old paths, follow after eminent holiness ourselves and recommend it boldly to others. This is the only way to be really happy.

Let us feel convinced, whatever others may say, that holiness is happiness, and that the man who gets through life most comfortably is the sanctified man. No doubt there are some true Christians who from ill health, or family trials, or other secret causes enjoy little sensible comfort and go mourning all their days on the way to heaven. But these are exceptional cases. As a general rule, in the long run of life, it will be found true that 'sanctified' people are the happiest people on earth! They have solid comforts which the world can neither give nor take away. The ways of wisdom are 'pleasant ways'; 'Great peace have those who love your law'; it was said by One who cannot lie: '... my yoke is easy and my burden is light'. But it is also written, 'There is no peace ... for the wicked' (Prov. 3:17; Ps. 119:165; Matt. 11:30; Isa. 48:22).

3

Holiness

'Without holiness no one will see the Lord'

(Heb. 12:14)

The text which heads this page opens up a subject of deep importance. That subject is *practical holiness*. It suggests a question which demands the attention of all professing Christians: Are *we* holy? Shall *we* see the Lord?

That question can never be out of season. The wise man tells us there is 'A time to weep and a time to laugh ... a time to be silent and a time to speak' (Eccl. 3:4,7), but there is no time, no, not a day in which a man ought not to be holy. Are we holy?

That question concerns all ranks and conditions of men. Some are rich and some are poor, some learned and some unlearned, some masters and some servants; but there is no rank or condition in life in which a man ought not to be holy. Are we holy?

I ask to be heard today about this question. How does the

account stand between our souls and God? In this hurrying, bustling world, let us stand still for a few minutes and consider the matter of holiness. I believe I might have chosen a subject more popular and pleasant. I am sure I might have found one more easy to handle. But I feel deeply I could not have chosen one more seasonable and more profitable to our souls. It is a solemn thing to hear the Word of God saying, 'without holiness no one will see the Lord'.

I will endeavour, by God's help, to examine *what* true holiness is and the reason *why* it is so needful. In conclusion, I will try to point out the *only way* in which holiness can be attained. Having considered the doctrinal side, let us now turn to the plain and *practical application*.

The nature of true practical holiness

First then, let me try to show what true practical holiness is. What sort of people are those whom God calls holy?

A man may go great lengths in religion – and yet never reach true holiness.

It is not *knowledge* – Balaam had that.

It is not *great profession* – Judas Iscariot had that.

It is not *doing many things* – Herod had that.

It is not *zeal for certain matters in religion* – Jehu had that.

It is not *morality and outward respectability of conduct* – the rich young ruler had that.

It is not *taking pleasure in hearing preachers* – the Jews in Ezekiel's time had that.

It is not *keeping company with godly people* – Joab and Gehazi and Demas had that.

Yet none of these were holy people. These things alone are not holiness. A man may have any one of them, and yet never see the Lord.

What then is true practical holiness? It is a hard question to answer. I do not mean that there is any lack of scriptural matter on the subject. But I fear lest I should give a defective view of holiness, and not say all that ought to be said – or lest I should say things about it that ought not to be said, and so do harm. Let me, however, try to draw a picture of biblical holiness that we may see it clearly before the eyes of our minds. Only let it never be forgotten, when I have said all, that my account is but a poor imperfect outline at the best.

1. Holiness is the habit of being of one mind with God, according as we find His mind described in Scripture. It is the habit of ...

agreeing in God's judgement,

hating what He hates,

loving what He loves, and

measuring everything in this world by the standard of His Word.

He who most entirely agrees with God – he is the most holy man.

2. A holy man will endeavour to shun every known sin, and to keep every known commandment. He will have ...

a decided bent of mind towards God,

a hearty desire to do His will,

a greater fear of displeasing Him than of displeasing the world,

and a love to all His ways.

He will feel what Paul felt when he said, 'For in my inner being I delight in God's law' (Rom. 7:22), and what David felt when he said, 'I consider all your precepts right, I hate every wrong path' (Ps. 119:128).

3. A holy man will strive to be like our Lord Jesus Christ. He will not only live the life of faith in Him and draw from Him all his daily peace and strength, but he will also labour to have the mind that was in Him, and to be conformed to His image (Rom. 8:29). It will be his aim ...

to bear with and forgive others, even as Christ forgave us;

to be unselfish, even as Christ pleased not Himself;

to walk in love, even as Christ loved us;

to be lowly minded and humble, even as Christ made Himself of no reputation and humbled Himself.

He will remember ...

that Christ was a faithful witness for the truth;

that He came not to do His own will;

that it was His food and drink to do His Father's will;

that He would continually deny Himself in order to minister to others;

that He was meek and patient under undeserved insults;

that He thought more of godly poor men than of kings;

that He was full of love and compassion to sinners;

that He was bold and uncompromising in denouncing sin;

that He sought not the praise of men, when He might have had it;

that He went about doing good;

that He was separate from worldly people;

that He continued in prayer;

that He would not let even His nearest relations stand in His way when God's work was to be done.

All these things, a holy man will try to remember. By them, he will endeavour to shape his course in life. He will lay to heart the saying of John: '... whoever claims to live in him [Christ] must live as Jesus did' (1 John 2:6); and the saying of Peter, that Christ 'suffered for you, leaving you an *example*, that you should follow in his steps' (1 Pet. 2:21, italics mine). Happy is he who has learned to make Christ his 'all', both for salvation and example! Much time would be saved, and much sin prevented, if men would oftener ask themselves the question: 'What would *Jesus* have said and done, if He were in my place?'

4. A holy man will follow after meekness, gentleness, patience, kind tempers and government of his tongue. He will bear much, forbear much, overlook much and be slow to talk of standing on *his rights*. We see a bright example of this in the behaviour of David when Shimei cursed him, and of Moses when Aaron and Miriam spoke against him (2 Sam. 16:10; Num. 12:3).

5. A holy man will follow after temperance and self-denial. He will labour ...

to mortify the desires of his body,

to crucify his flesh with his affections and lusts,

to curb his passions,

to restrain his carnal inclinations – lest at any time they break loose.

Oh, what a word is that of the Lord Jesus to the apostles:

'Be careful, or your hearts will be weighed down with carousing, drunkenness and the anxieties of life, and that day will close on you suddenly like a trap' (Luke 21:34); and that of the apostle Paul: 'I strike a blow to my *body* and make it my slave so that after I have preached to others, I myself will not be disqualified for the prize' (1 Cor. 9:27, italics mine).

6. A holy man will follow after love and brotherly kindness. He will endeavour to observe the 'golden rule' of *doing* as he would have men do to him, and *speaking* as he would have men speak to him. He will be full of affection towards his brethren, towards their bodies, their property, their characters, their feelings, their souls. '... whoever loves others,' says Paul, 'has fulfilled the law' (Rom. 13:8). He will abhor all lying, slandering, backbiting, cheating, dishonesty and unfair dealing – even in the least things. He will strive to adorn his religion by all his outward demeanour, and to make it lovely and beautiful in the eyes of all around him.

Alas, what condemning words are the thirteenth chapter of 1 Corinthians, and the Sermon on the Mount, when laid alongside the conduct of many professing Christians!

7. A holy man will follow after a spirit of mercy and benevolence towards others. He will not stand idle all the day. He will not be content with doing no harm – he will try to do good. He will strive to be useful in his day and generation, and to lessen the spiritual needs and misery around him as far as he can. Such was Dorcas: '... always doing good and helping the poor' – not merely *purposed* and *talked* about but *did*. Such a one was Paul: 'I will very gladly spend for you everything I have and expend myself as well,' he says. 'If I love you more, will you love me less?' (Acts 9:36; 2 Cor. 12:15).

8. A holy man will follow after purity of heart. He will dread all immorality and impurity of spirit, and seek to avoid all things that might draw him into it. He knows his own heart is like tinder, and will diligently keep clear of the sparks of temptation. Who shall dare to talk of their own strength – when David can fall?

There is many a hint to be gleaned from the ceremonial law. Under it the man who only *touched* a bone or a dead body or a grave or a diseased person became at once unclean in the sight of God. And these things were emblems and figures. Few Christians are ever too watchful and too particular about this point.

9. A holy man will follow after the fear of God. I do not mean the fear of a *slave* – who only works because he is afraid of punishment and would be idle if he did not dread discovery. I mean rather the fear of a *child* – who wishes to live and move as if he was always before his father's face, because he loves him.

What a noble example Nehemiah gives us of this! When he became governor at Jerusalem, he could have been supported by the Jews and required money from them for his sustenance. The former governors had done so. There was none to blame him, if he did. But he says, the 'earlier governors – those preceding me – placed a heavy burden on the people and took forty shekels of silver from them in addition to food and wine. Their assistants also lorded it over the people. But *out of reverence for God* I did not act like that' (Neh. 5:15, italics mine).

10. A holy man will follow after humility. He will desire, in lowliness of mind, to esteem all others better than himself. He will see more evil in his own heart than in any other in the world.

He will understand something of Abraham's feeling, when he says, 'I am dust and ashes!'

And Jacob's feeling, when he says, 'I am unworthy of the least of all Your mercies!'

And Job's feeling, when he says, 'Behold! I am vile!'

And Paul's feeling, when he says, 'I am the chief of sinners!'

Holy John Bradford, that faithful martyr of Christ, would sometimes finish his letters with these words: 'A most miserable sinner, John Bradford.'

The godly William Grimshaw's last words, when he lay on his deathbed, were these: 'Here goes an unprofitable servant!'

11. A holy man will follow after faithfulness in all the duties and relations in life. He will try not merely to fill his place as well as others, who take no thought for their souls, but even better because he has higher motives and more help than they. Those words of Paul should never be forgotten: 'Whatever you do, work at it with all your heart, as working for the Lord'; 'Never be lacking in zeal, but keep your spiritual fervour, serving the Lord' (Col. 3:23; Rom. 12:11).

Holy people should aim at *doing everything well* and should be ashamed of allowing themselves to do anything poorly, if they can help it. Like Daniel, they should seek to give no 'basis for charges' against themselves, except concerning the law of their God (Dan. 6:5). They should strive to be ...

good husbands and good wives,

good parents and good children,

good masters and good servants,

good neighbours,

good friends,

good subjects,

good in private and good in public,

good in the place of business and good by their firesides.

Holiness is worth little indeed if it does not bear this kind of fruit. The Lord Jesus puts a searching question to His people when He says, '… what are you doing *more than others*?' (Matt. 5:47, italics mine).

12. Last but not least, a holy man will follow after spiritual-mindedness. He will endeavour to set his affections on things above, and to hold things on earth with a very loose hand. He will not neglect the business of the present life, but the first place in his mind and thoughts will be given to eternal realities. He will aim to live like one whose treasure is in heaven, and to pass through this world like a stranger and pilgrim travelling to his home.

To commune with God in prayer, in the Bible and in the assembly of His people – these things will be the holy man's chief enjoyments. He will value every thing and place and company – just in proportion as it draws him nearer to God. He will enter into something of David's feeling, when he says, 'I cling to you'; 'You are my portion' (Ps. 63:8; 119:57).

Here let me insert that I am not without fear that my meaning will be mistaken, and the description I have given of holiness will discourage some tender conscience. I would not willingly make one righteous heart sad, or throw a stumbling block in any believer's way.

I do not say for a moment that holiness shuts out the presence of indwelling sin. No, far from it. It is the greatest misery of a holy man that he carries about with him a 'body of sin and death'; that often he would do good – but evil is present with him; that the old man is clogging all his movements and, as it were, trying to draw him back at every step he takes (Rom. 7:21).

But it is the excellence of a holy man that he is not at peace with indwelling sin, as others are. He hates it, mourns over it and longs to be free from its company. The work of sanctification within him is like the wall of Jerusalem – the building goes forward even 'in times of trouble' (Dan. 9:25).

Neither do I say that holiness comes to ripeness and perfection all at once; or that these graces I have touched on must be found in full bloom and vigour before you can call a man holy. No, far from it! Sanctification is always a progressive work. Some men's graces are in the blade, some in the ear and some are like full grain in the ear (Mark 4:28). All must have a beginning. We must never 'despise the day of small things' (Zech. 4:10).

Sanctification in the very holiest man is an imperfect work. The history of the brightest saints that ever lived will contain many a 'but' and 'however' and 'notwithstanding' before you reach the end. The gold will never be without some dross, the light will never shine without some clouds, until we reach the heavenly Jerusalem. The sun itself has spots upon its face. The holiest men have many a blemish and defect when weighed in the balance of the sanctuary. Their life is a continual warfare with sin, the world and the devil, and sometimes you will see them not overcoming – but overcome! The flesh is ever lusting against the spirit, and the spirit against the flesh. In many things we all stumble (Gal. 5:17; Jas. 3:2).

But still, for all this, I am sure that to have such a character as I have faintly drawn is the heart's desire and prayer of all true Christians. They press towards it – if they do not reach it. They may not attain to it – but they always aim at it. It is what they strive and labour to be – if it is not what they are.

And I do boldly and confidently say that *true holiness is a great reality*. It is something in a man that can be seen and known and marked and felt by all around him.

It is *light* – if it exists, it will show itself.

It is *salt* – if it exists, its savour will be perceived.

It is a *precious ointment* – if it exists, its fragrance cannot be hidden.

I am sure that we should make allowance for much backsliding, for much occasional deadness in professing Christians. I know a road may lead from one point to another, and yet have many a winding and turn. Just so, a man may be truly holy, and yet be drawn aside by many an infirmity. Gold is not the less gold because mingled with alloy; nor light the less light because faint and dim; nor grace the less grace because young and weak.

But after every allowance, I cannot see how any man deserves to be called 'holy' who wilfully allows himself in sins, and is not humbled and ashamed because of them. I dare not call anyone 'holy' who makes a habit of wilfully neglecting known duties and wilfully doing what he knows God has commanded him not to do. Well says Owen, 'He is no true believer, unto whom sin is not the greatest burden, sorrow, and trouble'!

Such are the leading characteristics of practical holiness. Let us examine ourselves and see whether we are acquainted with it. Let us prove our own selves.

The importance of practical holiness

Can holiness *save* us? Can holiness put away sin, cover iniquities, make satisfaction for transgressions, pay our debt to God? No, not a whit! God forbid that I should ever say so. Holiness can do none of these things. The brightest saints are all 'unprofitable servants' in themselves. Our purest works are no better than filthy rags when tried by the light of God's holy law. The white robe, which Jesus offers and faith puts on, must be our only righteousness; the name of Christ must be our only confidence; the Lamb's book of life must be our only title to heaven. With all our holiness we are no better than sinners. Our best things are stained and tainted with imperfection! They are all more or less incomplete, wrong in the motive, or defective in the performance. By the deeds of the law shall no child of Adam ever be justified. '... by *grace* you have been saved, through faith – and this is not from yourselves, it is the gift of God – not by works, so that no one can boast' (Eph. 2:8,9, italics mine).

Why then is holiness so important? Why does the apostle say, 'Without holiness, no man shall see the Lord'? Let me set out in order a few reasons.

1. For one thing, we must be holy, because the voice of God in Scripture plainly commands it. The Lord Jesus says to His people, 'unless your righteousness surpasses that of the Pharisees and the teachers of the law, you will certainly not enter the kingdom of heaven' (Matt. 5:20); 'Be perfect, therefore, as your heavenly Father is perfect' (Matt. 5:48). Paul tells the Thessalonians, 'It is God's will that you should be sanctified' (1 Thess. 4:3). And Peter says, 'But just as he who called you is holy, so be holy in all you do; for it is written: "Be holy, because I am holy"' (1 Pet. 1:15,16). 'In this,' says Leighton, 'law and gospel agree.'

2. We must be holy, because this is one grand end and purpose for which Christ came into the world. Paul writes to the Corinthians, 'he died for all, that those who live should no longer live for themselves but for him who died for them and was raised again' (2 Cor. 5:15); and to the Ephesians, 'Christ loved the church and gave himself up for her to make her holy, cleansing her' (Eph. 5:25,26); and to Titus, He 'gave himself for us to redeem us from all wickedness and to purify for himself a people that are his very own, eager to do what is good' (Titus 2:14). In short, to talk of men being saved from the guilt of sin without being at the same time saved from its dominion in their hearts is to contradict the witness of all Scripture.

Are believers said to be *elect*? It is 'through the sanctifying work of the Spirit'.

Are they *predestined*? It is 'to be conformed to the image of [God's] Son'.

Are they *chosen*? It is that they should be 'holy and blameless in his sight'.

Are they *called*? It is that they should live 'a holy life'.

Are they *afflicted*? It is that they 'may share in his holiness'.

Jesus is a complete Saviour. He does not merely take away the *guilt* of a believer's sin. He does more – He breaks its *power* (1 Pet. 1:2; Rom. 8:29; Eph. 1:4; 2 Tim. 1:9; Heb. 12:10).

3. We must be holy, because this is the only sound evidence that we have a saving faith in our Lord Jesus Christ. The twelfth Article of our church says truly that although good works cannot take away our sins, 'and endure the severity of God's judgment; yet are they pleasing and acceptable to God in Christ, and do spring out necessarily of a true and lively Faith insomuch that by them a lively Faith may be as evidently known as a tree discerned by the fruit'.

James warns us there is such a thing as a dead faith – a faith which goes no further than the profession of the lips, and has no influence on a man's character (Jas. 2:17). True saving faith is a very different kind of thing. True faith will always show itself by its fruits:

it will sanctify,

it will work by love,

it will overcome the world,

it will purify the heart.

I know that people are fond of talking about deathbed evidences. They will rest on words spoken in the hours of fear and pain and weakness, as if they might take comfort in them about the friends they lose. But I am afraid in ninety-nine cases out of a hundred such evidences are not to be depended on. I suspect that with rare exceptions *men die just as they have lived.*

The only safe evidence that we are one with Christ, and Christ in us, is holy life. Those who *live* unto the Lord are generally the only people who *die* in the Lord. If we would die the death of the righteous, let us not rest in slothful desires only; let us seek to live His life. It is a true saying of Traill's: 'That faith is unsound – whose *hopes of glory* do not purify his heart and life.'

4. We must be holy, because this is the only proof that we love the Lord Jesus Christ in sincerity. This is a point on which He has spoken most plainly, in the fourteenth and fifteenth chapters of John:

'If you love me, keep my commands'

'Whoever has my commands and keeps them is the one who loves me'

'Anyone who loves me will obey my teaching'

'You are my friends if you do what I command'

(John 14:15,21,23; 15:14). Plainer words than these, it would be difficult to find; and woe to those who neglect them.

Surely that man must be in an unhealthy state of soul, who can think of all that Jesus suffered and yet *loves those sins* for which that suffering was undergone!

It was sin which wove the crown of thorns!

It was sin which pierced our Lord's hands and feet and side!

It was sin which brought Him to Gethsemane and Calvary, to the cross and to the grave! Cold must our hearts be, if we do not hate sin and labour to get rid of it – though we may have to cut off the right hand and pluck out the right eye in doing it.

5. We must be holy, because this is the only sound evidence that we are true children of God. Children in this world are generally like their parents. Some, doubtless, are more so, and some less; but it is seldom indeed that you cannot trace a kind of family likeness.

And it is much the same with the children of God. The Lord Jesus says, 'If you were Abraham's children ... then you would do what Abraham did'; 'If God were your Father, you would love me' (John 8:39,42). If men have no likeness to the Father in heaven, it is vain to talk of their being His 'sons'. If we know nothing of holiness, we may flatter ourselves as we please, but we have not got the Holy Spirit dwelling in us. We are dead – and must be brought to life again; we are lost – and must be found. '... those who are led by the Spirit of God,' they and *they only* 'are the children of God' (Rom. 8:14).

We must show by our lives the family we belong to. We must let men see by our holy lives that we are indeed the children of the Holy One, or our sonship is but an empty name. 'Say not,' says Gurnall, 'that you have royal blood in your veins, and are born of God – unless you can prove your pedigree by daring to be holy!'

6. We must be holy, because this is the most likely way to do good to others. We cannot live to ourselves only, in this world. Our lives will always be doing either good or harm to those who see them. They are a silent sermon which all can read. It is sad indeed when they are a sermon for the devil's cause and not for God's.

I believe that far more is done for Christ's kingdom by the holy living of believers than we are at all aware of. There is a reality about such living which makes men feel, and obliges them to think. It carries a weight and influence with it which nothing else can give. It makes religion beautiful, and draws men to consider it, like a lighthouse seen afar off. The day of judgement will prove that many besides husbands have been 'won over without words' by a holy life (1 Pet. 3:1). You may *talk* to people about the doctrines of the gospel, and few will listen, and still fewer understand. But *your life* is an argument that none can escape! There is a meaning about holiness which not even the most unlearned can help understanding. They may not understand *justification* – but they can understand *love*.

I believe there is far more harm done by unholy and inconsistent professors than we are at all aware of. Such men are among Satan's best allies. They pull down by their lives what ministers build with their lips. They cause the chariot wheels of the gospel to drive heavily. They supply the children of this world with a never-ending excuse for remaining as they are. 'I cannot see the use of so much religion,' said an impious tradesman not long ago. 'I observe that some of my customers are always talking about the gospel and faith and election and the blessed promises and so forth – and yet these very people think nothing of cheating me of pence and halfpence when they have an opportunity. Now, if religious people can do such things, I do not see what good there is in religion.'

I grieve to be obliged to write such things, but I fear that Christ's name is too often blasphemed because of the lives of Christians. Let us take heed lest the blood of souls should be required at our hands. From murder of souls by inconsistency and loose walking, good Lord, deliver us! Oh, for the sake of others, if for no other reason, let us strive to be holy.

7. We must be holy, because our present comfort depends much upon it. We are sadly apt to forget that there is a close connection between ...

sin – and sorrow,

holiness – and happiness,

sanctification – and consolation.

God has so wisely ordered it, that our well-*being* and our well-*doing* are linked together. He has mercifully provided that even in this world, it shall be in man's best interest to be holy. Our justification is not by works, our calling and election are not according to our works; but it is vain for anyone to suppose that he will have a lively sense of his justification or an assurance of his calling so long as he neglects good works, or does not strive to live a holy life. 'We know that we have come to know him if we keep his commands'; 'This is how we know that we belong to the truth and how we set our hearts at rest' (1 John 2:3; 3:19).

A believer may as soon expect to feel the sun's rays upon a dark and cloudy day as to feel strong consolation in Christ while he does not follow Him fully. When the disciples forsook the Lord and fled, they escaped danger, but they were miserable and sad. When, shortly after, they confessed Him boldly before men, they were cast into prison and beaten, but we are told they *rejoiced* 'because they had been counted worthy of suffering disgrace for the Name' (Acts 5:41). Oh, for our own sakes, if there were no other reason – let us strive to be holy! He who follows Jesus most *fully* will always follow Him most comfortably!

8. Lastly, we must be holy, because without holiness on earth we will never be prepared to enjoy heaven.

Heaven is a holy *place*.

The Lord of heaven is a holy *Being*.

The angels are holy *creatures*.

Holiness is written on everything in heaven. The book of

Revelation says expressly, 'Nothing impure will ever enter it, nor will anyone who does what is shameful or deceitful, but only those whose names are written in the Lamb's book of life' (Rev. 21:27).

How will we ever be at home and happy in heaven – if we die unholy? Death works no change in our essential character. The grave makes no alteration. Each will rise again with the same character in which he breathed his last. Where will our place be in eternity – if we are strangers to holiness now?

Suppose for a moment that you were allowed to enter heaven without holiness. What would you do? What possible enjoyment could you feel there? To which of all the saints would you join yourself, and by whose side would you sit down? Their *pleasures* are not your pleasures, their *tastes* not your tastes, their *character* not your character. How could you possibly be happy, if you had not been holy on earth?

Now perhaps, you love the company of ...

the light and the careless,

the worldly minded and the covetous,

the reveller and the pleasure-seeker,

the ungodly and the profane.

There will be none such in heaven.

Now perhaps you think the saints of God too strict and particular and serious. You rather avoid them. You have no delight in their society. There will be no other company in heaven.

Now perhaps you think that praying and Scripture-reading and hymn-singing are dull and melancholy and foolish work, a thing to be tolerated now and then – but not enjoyed. You reckon the Sabbath a burden and a weariness; you could not possibly spend more than a small part of it in worshipping God. But remember, heaven is a never-ending Sabbath. The inhabitants thereof rest not day or night, saying, 'Holy, holy, holy, Lord God Almighty' and singing the praise of the Lamb. How could an unholy man find pleasure in occupation such as this?

Do you think that such a one would delight to meet David and Paul and John – after a life spent in doing the very things they spoke against? Would he take sweet counsel with them and find that he and they had much in common? Do you think, above all, that he would rejoice to meet Jesus, the crucified One, face to face – after cleaving to the sins for which He died, after loving His enemies and despising His friends? Would he stand before Him with confidence, and join in the cry, 'this is our God; we trusted in him ... let us rejoice and be glad in his salvation' (Isa. 25:9)? Do you not think, rather, that the tongue of an unholy man would cleave to the roof of his mouth with shame, and his only desire would be to be cast out? He would feel a stranger in a land he did not know, a black sheep amid Christ's holy flock. The voice of cherubim and seraphim, the song of angels and archangels and all the company of heaven would be a language he could not understand. The very *air* would seem an air he could not breathe!

I do not know what others may think – but to me it does seem clear that *heaven would be a miserable place to an unholy man*. It cannot be otherwise. People may say in a vague way that they 'hope to go to heaven', but they do not consider what they say. There must be a certain '*fitness* for the inheritance of the saints in light'. Our hearts must be somewhat in tune. To reach the holiday of glory we must pass through the training school of grace. We must be heavenly minded and have heavenly tastes in the present life – or else we will never find ourselves in heaven in the life to come!

And now, before I go any further, let me say a few words by way of ...

Application

1. The most pertinent question to ask is this: 'Are *you* holy?' Listen, I beg you, to the question I put to you this day. Do *you* know anything of the holiness of which I have been speaking?

I do not ask whether you attend your church regularly, whether you have been baptized and received the Lord's Supper, whether you have the *name* of Christian. I ask something more than all this: Are you holy – or are you not?

I do not ask whether you approve of holiness in others, whether you like to read the lives of holy people and to talk of holy things and to have on your table holy books, whether you mean to be holy and hope you will be holy some day. I ask something further: are you yourself holy this very day – or are you not?

And why do I ask so straightly and press the question so strongly? I do it because the Scripture says, 'without holiness no one will see the Lord'. It is written – it is not my imagination; it is the Bible – not my private opinion; it is the Word of God – not of man: 'without holiness no one will see the Lord'.

Alas, what searching, sifting words are these! What thoughts come across my mind as I write them down! I look at the *world* and see the greater part of it lying in wickedness. I look at *professing Christians* and see the vast majority having nothing of Christianity but the name. I turn to the Bible, and I hear the Spirit saying, 'without holiness no one will see the Lord'!

Surely it is a text that ought to make us consider our ways and search our hearts. Surely it should raise within us solemn thoughts and send us to prayer.

You may try to put me off by saying you feel much and think much about these things – far more than many suppose. I answer, 'This is not the point. The poor lost souls in hell do as much as this! The great question is not what you *think*, and what you *feel* – but what you *do*.'

You may say, it was never meant that *all* Christians should be holy, and that holiness, such as I have described, is only for great saints and people of uncommon gifts. I answer, 'I cannot see that in Scripture. I read that *every* man who has hope in Christ purifies himself' (1 John 3:3). Without holiness *no man* shall see the Lord.

You may say, it is impossible to be so holy and to do our duty in this life at the same time; the thing cannot be done. I answer, 'You are mistaken.' It can be done. With Christ on your side, nothing is impossible. It has been done by many. David and Obadiah and Daniel are all examples that go to prove it.

You may say, if you were so holy you would be unlike other people. I answer, 'I know it well. It is just what you ought to be. Christ's true servants always were unlike the world around them – a separate nation, a peculiar people – and you must be so too, if you would be saved.'

You may say, at this rate, very few will be saved. I answer, 'I know it. It is precisely what we are told in the Sermon on the Mount.' The Lord Jesus said so 1,800 years ago. '... small is the gate and narrow the road that leads to life, and only a *few* find it' (Matt. 7:14, italics mine). Few will be saved, because few will take the trouble to seek salvation. Men will not deny themselves the pleasures of sin, and their own way, for a little season. They turn their backs on a priceless inheritance – 'an inheritance that can never perish, spoil or fade. This inheritance is kept in heaven for you' (1 Pet. 1:4); 'You will not come to Me,' says Jesus, 'that you might have life' (see John 5:40).

You may say, these are hard sayings; the way is *very narrow*. I answer, 'I know it. So says the Sermon on the Mount.' The Lord Jesus always said that men must take up the cross daily, and that they must be ready to cut off hand or foot, if they would be His disciples. It is in religion, as it is in other things – there are no gains without pains. That which costs nothing – is worth nothing!

Whatever we may think fit to say, we must be holy if we would see the Lord in glory. Where is our Christianity, if we are not holy? We must not merely have a Christian *name* and Christian *knowledge* – we must have a Christian *character* also. We must be saints on *earth* if ever we mean to be saints in *heaven*. God has said it, and He will not go back: '... without holiness no one will see the Lord'.

'The pope's calendar,' says Jenkyn, 'only makes saints of the *dead* – but Scripture requires sanctity in the *living*.' 'Let not men deceive themselves,' says Owen, 'sanctification is a qualification indispensably necessary unto those who will be under the conduct of the Lord Christ unto salvation. He leads none to Heaven – but whom He sanctifies on the earth. This living Head, will not admit of dead members!'

Surely we need not wonder that Scripture says, 'You must be born again' (John 3:7). Surely it is as clear as noonday that many *professing* Christians need a complete change, new hearts, new natures, if ever they are to be saved. Old things must pass away;

they must become new creatures. 'Without holiness no one' – be he who he may – 'no one will see the Lord!'

2. Let me speak a little to *believers*. I ask you this question, 'Do you think you feel the *importance* of holiness as much as you should?'

I admit that I fear the temper of the times about this subject. I doubt exceedingly whether holiness holds that place which it deserves in the thoughts and attention of some of the Lord's people. I would humbly suggest that we are apt to overlook the doctrine of growth in grace, and that we do not sufficiently consider how very far a person may go in a profession of religion and yet have no grace, and be dead in God's sight after all! I believe that Judas Iscariot seemed very like the other apostles. When the Lord warned them that one would betray Him, no one said, 'Is it Judas?' We had better think more about the churches of Sardis and Laodicea than we do.

I have no desire to make an idol of holiness. I do not wish to dethrone Christ – and put holiness in His place. But I must candidly say, I wish that sanctification was more thought of in this day than it seems to be, and I therefore take occasion to press the subject on all believers into whose hands these pages may fall. I fear that it is sometimes forgotten that God has married together justification and sanctification. They are distinct and different things, beyond question, but one is never found without the other. All justified people are sanctified, and all sanctified people are justified. What God has joined together let no man dare to put asunder.

Tell me not of your justification, unless you have also some marks of sanctification. Boast not of *Christ's* work for you – unless you can show us the *Spirit's* work in you. Do not think that Christ and the

Spirit can ever be divided. I do not doubt that many believers know these things, but I think it good for us to be put in remembrance of them. Let us prove that we know them, by our lives. Let us try to keep in view this text more continually: 'Make every effort to ... be holy; without holiness no one will see the Lord' (Heb. 12:14)!

I must frankly say that the overly sensitive approach many people take towards the subject of holiness is a dangerous error. Some would think it more dangerous to approach the subject, yet the opposite is the case! Yet if we exalt Christ as the 'way, the truth and the life', how can we refuse to speak strongly about those who call themselves after His name?

I would say it with all reverence – but say it I must: I sometimes fear that if Christ were on earth now, there are many who would think His preaching to be *legal*. And if Paul were writing his epistles, there are those who would think he had better not write the latter part of most of them as he did. But let us remember that the Lord Jesus did speak the Sermon on the Mount, and that the epistle to the Ephesians contains *six* chapters and not *four*. I grieve to feel obliged to speak in this way – but I am sure there is a cause.

That great divine, John Owen, the Dean of Christ Church, used to say, more than two hundred years ago, that there were people whose whole religion seemed to consist in going about complaining of their own corruptions and telling everyone that they could do nothing of themselves. I am afraid that after two centuries, the same thing might be said with truth of some of Christ's *professing* people in this day. I know there are texts in Scripture which warrant such complaints. I do not object to them, when they come from men who walk in the steps of the apostle Paul and fight a good fight, as he did, against sin, the devil and the world. But I never like such complaints when I see ground for suspecting, as I often do, that they are only a cloak to cover spiritual laziness, and an excuse for spiritual sloth. If we say with Paul, 'What a wretched man I am!' let us also be able to say with him, 'I press on towards the goal'. Let us not quote his example in one thing while we do not follow him in another (Rom. 7:24; Phil. 3:14).

I do not set up myself to be better than other people; and if anyone asks, 'What are you, that you write in this way?' I answer, 'I am a very poor creature indeed.' But I say that I cannot read the Bible without desiring to see many believers ...

more *spiritual*,

more *holy*,

more *single-eyed*,

more *heavenly minded*,

more *wholehearted*,

than they are in the nineteenth century. I want to see among believers ...

more of a *pilgrim spirit*,

a more decided *separation* from the world,

a conversation more evidently in heaven,

a closer walk with God –

and therefore I have written as I have.

Is it true, that we need a higher standard of personal holiness in this day? Where is our patience? Where is our zeal? Where is our love? Where are our works? Where is the *power* of religion to be seen, as it was in times gone by? Where is that unmistakable *tone* which used to distinguish the saints of old and shake the world?

Truly our silver has become dross, our wine mixed with water and our salt has very little savour. We are all more than half asleep! The night is far spent, and the day is at hand. Let us awake – and sleep no more. Let us open our eyes more widely than we have done up to this time. '... let us throw off everything that hinders and the sin that so easily entangles'; '... let us purify ourselves from everything that contaminates body and spirit, perfecting holiness out of reverence for God' (Heb. 12:1; 2 Cor. 7:1). 'Did Christ die,' says Owen, 'and shall sin live? Was He crucified in the world — and shall our affections to the world be quick and lively? Oh, where is the spirit of Paul, who by the cross of Christ was crucified to the world, and the world to him?'

3. A word of advice. Would you be holy? Would you become a new creature? Then you must *begin with Christ*. You will do just nothing at all, and make no progress until you feel your sin and weakness, and flee to Him. He is the *root* and *beginning* of all holiness, and the way to be holy is to come to Him by faith and be joined to Him. Christ is not wisdom and righteousness only to His people – but sanctification also. Men sometimes try to make themselves holy first of all, and sad work they make of it. They toil and labour and turn over many new leaves, and make many changes, and yet they are like the woman with the issue of blood before she came to Christ, who 'instead of getting better ... grew worse' (Mark 5:26). They run in vain and labour in vain, and little wonder, for they are beginning at the wrong end. They are building up a wall of sand; their work runs down as fast as they throw it up. They are baling water out of a leaky vessel; the leak gains on them – not they on the leak.

Other foundation of holiness can no man lay than that which Paul laid – even Christ Jesus. Without Christ we can do nothing (John 15:5). It is a strong but true saying of Traill's:

> Wisdom out of Christ is damning folly;
> righteousness out of Christ is guilt and condemnation;
> sanctification out of Christ is filth and sin;
> redemption out of Christ is bondage and slavery!

Do you want to attain holiness? Do you feel this day a real hearty desire to be holy? Would you be a partaker of the divine nature? Then go to Christ! Wait for nothing. Wait for nobody. Linger not. Do not think to make yourself ready. Go and say to Him, in the words of that beautiful hymn:

> Nothing in my hand I bring,
> Simply to Thy cross I cling;
> Naked, come to Thee for dress;
> Helpless, look to Thee for grace ...

There is not a brick nor a stone laid in the work of our sanctification – until we go to Christ. Holiness is His special *gift* to His believing people. Holiness is the *work* He carries on in their hearts by the Spirit whom He puts within them. He is appointed a 'Prince and Saviour that he might bring [them] to repentance and forgive their sins'. To as many as receive Him, He gives power to become sons of God (Acts 5:31; see John 1:12,13). Holiness comes not by blood – parents cannot give it to their children; nor of the will of the flesh – man cannot produce it in himself; nor of the will of man – ministers cannot give it to you by baptism. Holiness comes from Christ. It is the *result* of vital union with Him. It is the *fruit* of being a living branch of the true Vine. Go then to Christ and say, 'Lord, not only save me from the *guilt* of sin – but send the Spirit, whom You promised, and save me from its *power*. Make me holy. Teach me to do Your will.'

Would you continue holy? Then abide in Christ (John 15:4,5). It pleased the Father that in Him should all fullness dwell – a full supply for all a believer's needs. He is the *Physician* to whom you must daily go, if you would keep well. He is the *Manna* which you must daily eat, and the *Rock* from which you must daily drink. His arm is the arm on which you must daily lean, as you come up out of the wilderness of this world. You must not only be rooted – you must also be built up in Him.

Paul was a man of God indeed, a holy man, a growing thriving Christian – and what was the secret of it all? He was one to whom Christ was *all in all*. He was ever looking unto Jesus. 'I can do all this,' he says, 'through him who gives me strength'; 'I no longer live, but Christ lives in me. The life I now live ... I live by faith in the Son of God'. Let us go and do likewise (Phil. 4:13; Gal. 2:20).

May all who read these pages know these things by experience – and not by hearsay only! May we all feel the importance of holiness far more than we have ever done yet! May our years be holy years with our souls – and then they will be happy ones! Whether we live – may we live unto the Lord; or whether we die – may we die unto the Lord. And if He comes for us – may we be found in peace, without spot, and blameless!

4

The Fight

'Fight the good fight of the faith'

(1 Tim. 6:12)

It is a curious fact that there is no subject about which most people feel such deep interest as fighting. Young men and maidens, old men and little children, high and low, rich and poor, learned and unlearned – all feel a deep interest in wars, battles and fighting.

A simple inscrutable fact presents itself to us – we are excited when we hear stories of war. Some would consider an Englishman rather boring, if he cared nothing about the story of Waterloo or Inkerman or Balaclava or Lucknow. Many consider the heart cold and stupid which is not moved and thrilled by the struggles at Sedan and Strasburg and Metz and Paris during the war between France and Germany.

But there is another warfare of far greater importance than any war that was ever waged by man. It is a warfare which concerns not two or three nations only, but every Christian man and woman born into the world. The warfare I speak of is the *spiritual* warfare. It is the fight which everyone who would be saved must fight about his soul.

This warfare, I am aware, is a thing of which many know nothing. Talk to them about it, and they are ready to set you down as a madman, an enthusiast or a fool! And yet it is as real and true as any war the world has ever seen. It has its hand-to-hand conflicts – and its wounds. It has its watchings – and fatigues. It has its sieges – and assaults. It has its victories – and its defeats. Above all, it has *consequences* which are solemn, tremendous and most peculiar. In earthly warfare, the consequences to nations are often temporary and remediable. In the spiritual warfare, it is very different. Of that warfare, the consequences, when the fight is over, are unchangeable and eternal.

It is of this warfare that Paul spoke to Timothy, when he wrote those burning words, 'Fight the good fight of the faith. Take hold of the eternal life' (1 Tim. 6:12). It is of this warfare that I propose to speak in this message. I hold the subject to be closely connected with that of sanctification and holiness. He who would understand the nature of true holiness must know that the Christian is 'a man of war'. If we would be holy – we must fight!

1. True Christianity is a *fight*

True Christianity! Let us mind that word 'true'. There is a vast quantity of religion current in the world which is not true, genuine Christianity. It passes muster, it satisfies sleepy consciences, but it is not good money. It is not the authentic reality that called itself Christianity in the beginning. There are thousands of men and women who go to churches and chapels every Sunday and call themselves Christians. They make a 'profession' of faith in Christ. Their names are in the baptismal register. They are reckoned Christians while they live. They are married with a Christian marriage service. They mean to be buried as Christians when they die.

But you never see any 'fight' about their religion! Of spiritual strife and exertion and conflict and self-denial and watching and warring they know literally nothing at all. Such Christianity may satisfy man, and those who say anything against it may be thought very hard and uncharitable, but it certainly is not the Christianity of the Bible. It is not the religion which the Lord Jesus founded and His apostles preached. It is not the religion which produces real holiness. True Christianity is 'a fight'!

The true Christian is called to be a *soldier*, and must behave as such from the day of his conversion to the day of his death. He is not meant to live a life of pious ease, indolence and security. He must never imagine for a moment that he can sleep and doze along the way to heaven, like one travelling in an easy carriage. If he takes his standard of Christianity from the people of this world, he may be content with such vain notions — but he will find no countenance for them in the Word of God. If the Bible is the rule of his faith and practice, he will find his course laid down very plainly in this matter. He must 'fight'.

With *whom* is the Christian soldier meant to fight? Not with other Christians. Wretched indeed is that man's idea of religion, who imagines that it consists in perpetual controversy! He who is never satisfied unless he is engaged in some strife between church and church, chapel and chapel, sect and sect, faction and faction, party and party, knows nothing yet as he ought to know. As a general rule, the cause of sin is never so much helped as when Christians waste their strength in quarrelling with one another, and spend their time in petty squabbles.

No, indeed! The principal fight of the Christian is with ...

the world,

the flesh and

the devil.

These are his never-dying foes! These are the three chief enemies against whom he must wage war. Unless he gets the victory over these three, all other victories are useless and vain. If he had a nature like an angel, and were not a fallen creature, the warfare would not be so essential. But with a corrupt heart, a busy devil and an ensnaring world, he must either 'fight' or be lost.

He must fight the *flesh*. Even after conversion, he carries within him a nature prone to evil and a heart weak and unstable as water. That heart will never be free from imperfection in this world, and it is a miserable delusion to expect it.

To keep that heart from going astray, the Lord Jesus bids us 'Watch and pray'. The spirit may be ready, but the flesh is weak. There is need of a daily struggle and a daily wrestling in prayer. 'I keep my body under control,' cries Paul, 'and bring it into subjection'; 'I see another law at work in me, waging war against the law of my mind and making me a prisoner ... What a wretched man I am! Who will recuse me from this body that is subject to death?'; 'Those who belong to Christ Jesus have crucified the flesh with its passions and desires'; 'Put to death ... whatever belongs to your earthly nature' (Mark 14:38; see 1 Cor. 9:27; Rom. 7:23,24; Gal. 5:24; Col. 3:5).

He must fight the *world*. The subtle influence of that mighty enemy must be daily resisted, and without a daily battle can never be overcome.

The love of the world's good things,

the fear of the world's laughter or blame,

the secret desire to keep in with the world,

the secret wish to do as others in the world do, and not to run into extremes – all these are spiritual foes which beset the Christian continually on his way to heaven, and must be conquered. '... friendship with the world means enmity against God ... anyone who chooses to be a friend of the world becomes an enemy of God'; 'If anyone loves the world, love for the Father is not in them'; '... the world has been crucified to me, and I to the world'; '... everyone born of God overcomes the world'; 'Do not conform to the pattern of this world' (Jas. 4:4; 1 John 2:15; Gal. 6:14; 1 John 5:4; Rom. 12:2).

He must fight the *devil*. That old enemy of mankind is not dead. Ever since the Fall of Adam and Eve, he has been 'roaming throughout the earth, going to and fro on it' (Job 1:7), and striving to compass one great end – the ruin of man's soul. Never slumbering and never sleeping, he is always going about as a 'lion looking for someone to devour' (1 Pet. 5:8). An unseen enemy, he is always near us, about our path and about our bed, and spying out all our ways. A murderer and a liar from the beginning (John 8:44), he labours night and day to cast us down to hell. Sometimes by leading into superstition, sometimes by suggesting infidelity, sometimes by one kind of tactics and sometimes by another – he is always carrying on a campaign against our souls. 'Satan has asked to sift all of you as wheat' (Luke 22:31).

This mighty adversary must be daily resisted if we wish to be saved. But 'this kind goes not out' but by watching and praying and fighting and putting on the whole armour of God. The strong man armed will never be kept out of our hearts, without a daily battle (Eph. 6:11).

Some may think these statements too strong. You imagine that I am going too far, and laying on the colours too thickly. You are secretly saying to yourself that men and women may surely get to heaven without all this trouble and warfare and fighting. Listen to me for a few minutes, and I will show you that I have something to say on God's behalf. Remember the maxim of the wisest general that ever lived in England: 'In time of war, it is the worst mistake to underrate your enemy, and try to make a little war.'

This Christian warfare is no light matter. What says the Scripture? 'Fight the good fight of the faith. Take hold of the eternal life'; endure hardship 'like a good soldier of Christ Jesus'; 'Put on the full armour of God, so that you can take your stand against the devil's schemes. For our struggle is not against flesh and blood, but against the rulers, against the authorities, against the powers of this dark world and against the spiritual forces of evil in the heavenly realms. Therefore put on the full armour of God, so that when the day of evil comes, you may be able to stand your ground, and after you have done everything, to stand'; 'Make every effort to enter through the narrow door'; 'Be on your guard; stand firm in the faith; be courageous; be strong'; '... fight the battle well, holding on to faith and a good conscience' (1 Tim. 6:12; 2 Tim. 2:3; Eph. 6:11–13; Luke 13:24; 1 Cor. 16:13; 1 Tim. 1:18,19).

Words such as these appear to me clear, plain and unmistakable.

They all teach one and the same great lesson, if we are willing to receive it. That lesson is that true Christianity is a struggle, a fight and a warfare. He who pretends to condemn 'fighting' and teaches that we ought to sit still and 'yield ourselves to God' appears to me to misunderstand his Bible, and to make a great mistake.

One thing is certain – this Christian warfare is a great reality and a subject of vast importance. It is not a matter like church government and ceremonials, about which men may differ and yet reach heaven at last. Necessity is laid upon us. *We must fight.* There are no promises in the Lord Jesus Christ's epistles to the seven churches, except to those who 'overcome'. Where there is grace there will be conflict. The believer is a soldier. There is no holiness without a warfare. Saved souls will always be found to have fought a fight.

It is a fight of *absolute necessity*. Let us not think that in this war we can remain neutral and sit still. Such a line of action may be possible in the strife of nations, but it is utterly impossible in that conflict which concerns the soul. The plan of keeping quiet and letting things alone – this will never do in the Christian warfare. Here, at any rate, no one can escape serving under the plea that he is 'a man of peace'. To be at peace with the world, the flesh and the devil is to be at enmity with God and in the broad way that leads to destruction. We have no choice or option. We must either fight or be lost!

It is a fight of *universal necessity*. No rank or class or age can plead exemption, or escape the battle. Ministers and people, preachers and hearers, old and young, high and low, rich and poor, gentle and simple, kings and subjects, landlords and tenants, learned and unlearned – all alike must carry arms and go to *war*. All have by nature a heart full of pride, unbelief, sloth, worldliness and sin. All are living in a world beset with snares, traps and pitfalls for the soul. All have near them a busy, restless, malicious devil. All, from the queen in her palace down to the pauper in the workhouse – all must fight, if they would be saved.

It is a fight of *perpetual necessity*. It admits of no breathing time, no armistice, no truce. On weekdays as well as on Sundays, in private as well as in public, at home by the family fireside as well as abroad, in little things, like management of tongue and temper, as well as in great ones, like the government of kingdoms – the Christian's warfare must unceasingly go on. The foe we have to do with keeps no holidays, never slumbers and never sleeps. So long as we have breath in our bodies, we must keep on our armour and remember that we are on an enemy's ground. 'Even on the brink of Jordan,' said a dying saint, 'I find Satan nibbling at my heels!' *We must fight until we die!*

Let us consider well these propositions. Let us take care that our own religion is real, genuine and true. The saddest symptom about many so-called Christians is the utter absence of anything like conflict and fight in their Christianity. They eat, they drink, they dress, they work, they amuse themselves, they get money, they spend money, they go through a scanty round of formal religious services once or twice every week. But of the great spiritual warfare – its watchings and strugglings, its agonies and anxieties, its battles and contests – of all this they appear to know nothing at all. Let us take care that this case is not our own. The worst state of soul is when the strong man armed keeps the house, and his goods are at peace, when he leads men and women captive at his will, and they make no resistance. The worst chains are those which are neither felt nor seen by the prisoner (Luke 11:21; 2 Tim. 2:26).

We may take comfort about our souls, if we know anything of an inward fight and conflict. It is the invariable companion of genuine Christian holiness. It is not everything, I am well aware – but it is something. Do we find in our heart of hearts a spiritual struggle? Do we feel anything of the flesh warring against the spirit, and the spirit against the flesh, so that we cannot do the things we would (Gal. 5:17)? Are we conscious of *two principles* within us, contending for the mastery? Do we feel anything of war in our inward man? Well, let us thank God for it! It is a good sign. It is strongly probable evidence of the great work of sanctification.

All true saints are soldiers. Anything is better than apathy, stagnation, deadness and indifference! We are in a better state than many. The most part of so-called Christians have no feeling at all.

We are evidently no friends of Satan. Like the kings of this world, he wars not against his own subjects. The very fact that he assaults us should fill our minds with hope. I say again, let us take comfort. The child of God has two great marks about him, and of these two, we have one. He may be known by his inward warfare – as well as by his inward peace.

2. True Christianity is the fight *of faith*

Unlike the battles of the world, true Christianity fights in a realm that does not depend upon physical strength, the strong arm, the quick eye or the swift foot. Conventional weaponry does not come into play. Rather, its weapons are spiritual – and faith is the axis upon which the battle turns.

A *general faith in the truth of God's written Word* is the primary foundation of the Christian soldier's character. He ...

is what he is,

does what he does,

thinks as he thinks,

acts as he acts,

hopes as he hopes,

behaves as he behaves –

for one simple reason – he believes certain propositions revealed and laid down in Holy Scripture. '... anyone who comes to [God] must believe that he exists and that he rewards those who earnestly seek him' (Heb. 11:6).

A religion without doctrine is a thing which many are fond of talking of in the present day. It sounds very fine at first. It looks very pretty at a distance. But the moment we sit down to examine and consider it, we shall find it a simple impossibility. We might as well talk of a body without bones and sinews. No man will ever be anything or do anything in religion – unless he sincerely believes something. Even those who profess to hold the miserable and uncomfortable views of the deists are obliged to confess that they believe something. With all their bitter sneers against dogmatic theology and Christian credulity, as they call it, they themselves have a kind of faith.

As for true Christians, faith is the very backbone of their spiritual existence. No one ever fights earnestly against the world, the flesh and the devil unless he has engraved on his heart certain great principles which he believes. What they are, he may hardly know and may certainly not be able to define or write down. But there they are and, consciously or unconsciously, they form the roots of his religion. Wherever you see a man, whether rich or poor, learned or unlearned, wrestling manfully with sin and trying to overcome it, you may be sure there are certain great principles which that man believes. The poet who wrote the famous lines

> For modes of faith let graceless zealots fight,
> His can't be wrong whose life is in the right.

was a clever man, but a poor theologian. There is no such thing as right *living* – without *faith* and *believing*.

A *special faith in our Lord Jesus Christ's person, work and office* is the life, heart and mainspring of the Christian soldier's character.

He sees by faith an unseen Saviour, who ...

loved him,

gave Himself for him,

paid his debts for him,

bore his sins, carried his transgressions,

rose again for him, and

appears in heaven for him as his Advocate at the right hand of God.

He sees Jesus – and clings to Him. Seeing this Saviour and trusting in Him, he feels peace and hope and willingly does battle against the foes of his soul.

He sees ...

his own many sins,

his own weak heart,

a tempting world,

a busy devil –

and if he looked only at them, he might well despair. But he sees also a mighty Saviour, an interceding Saviour, a sympathizing Saviour – His blood, His righteousness, His everlasting priesthood – and he believes that all this is his own. He sees Jesus, and casts his whole weight on Him. Seeing Him, he cheerfully fights on, with a full confidence that he will prove more than conqueror through Him that loved him (Rom. 8:37).

Habitual lively faith in Christ's presence and readiness to help is the secret of the Christian soldier fighting successfully.

It must never be forgotten that *faith admits of degrees*. All men do not believe alike, and even the same person has his ebbs and flows of faith and believes more heartily at one time than another. According to the *present degree* of his faith, the Christian ...

fights well – or ill,

wins victories – or suffers occasional repulses,

comes off triumphant – or loses a battle.

He who has the most faith will always be the happiest and most comfortable soldier. Nothing makes the anxieties of warfare sit so lightly on a man as the assurance of Christ's love and continual protection. Nothing enables him to bear the fatigue of watching, struggling and wrestling against sin like the confidence that the indwelling Christ is on his side, and success is sure.

It is the 'shield of faith' which quenches all the fiery darts of the wicked one (Eph. 6:16). It is the man who can say, 'I know whom I have believed' who can say in time of suffering, I have 'no cause for shame' (2 Tim. 1:12). He who wrote those glowing words: 'Therefore we do not lose heart ... our light and momentary troubles are achieving for us an eternal glory that far outweights them all' (2 Cor. 4:16,17) was the man who wrote with the same pen, 'So we fix our eyes not on what is seen, but on what is unseen, since what is seen is temporary, but what is unseen is eternal' (2 Cor. 4:18). It is the man who said, 'I live by faith in the Son of God' who said, in the same epistle, 'the world has been crucified to me, and I to the world' (Gal. 2:20; 6:14). It is the man who said, 'to me, to live is Christ' who said, in the same epistle, 'I have learned to be content whatever the circumstances' and 'I can do all this through him who gives me strength' (Phil. 1:21; 4:11,13). The more faith – the more victory! The more faith – the more inward peace!

I think it is impossible to overrate the value and importance of faith. Well may the apostle Peter call it 'precious' (2 Pet. 1:1). Time would fail me if I tried to recount a hundredth part of the victories which by faith Christian soldiers have obtained.

Let us take down our Bibles and read with attention the eleventh chapter of the epistle to the Hebrews. Let us mark the long list of worthies whose names are thus recorded, from Abel down to Moses, even before Christ was born of the virgin Mary, and brought life and immortality into full light by the gospel. Let us note well what battles they won against the world, the flesh and the devil. And then let us remember that believing did it all. These men looked forward to the promised Messiah. They saw Him who is invisible. '... faith ... is what the ancients were commended for' (Heb. 11:1,2).

Let us turn to the pages of early church history. Let us see how the primitive Christians held fast their religion even unto death, and were not shaken by the fiercest persecutions of heathen emperors. For centuries there were never lacking men like Polycarp and Ignatius, who were ready to die rather than deny Christ. Fines and prisons and torture and fire and sword were unable to crush the spirit of the noble army of martyrs. The whole power of imperial Rome, the mistress of the world, proved unable to stamp out the religion which began with a few fishermen and publicans in Palestine! And then let us remember that believing in an unseen Jesus was the church's strength. They won their victory by faith.

Let us examine the story of the Protestant Reformation. Let us study the lives of its leading champions, Wycliffe and Huss and Luther and Ridley and Latimer and Hooper. Let us mark how these gallant soldiers of Christ stood firm against a host of adversaries and were ready to die for their principles. What battles they fought! What controversies they maintained! What persecution they endured! What tenacity of purpose they exhibited against a world in arms! And then let us remember that *believing in an unseen Jesus* was the secret of their strength. They overcame by faith.

Let us consider the men who have made the greatest marks in church history in the last 100 years. Let us observe how men like Wesley and Whitefield and Venn and Romaine stood alone in their day and generation and revived English religion in the face of opposition from men high in office and in the face of slander, ridicule and persecution from nine-tenths of *professing* Christians in our land. Let us mark how these noble witnesses never flinched to the end, and won the respect even of their worst adversaries. And then let us remember that *believing in an unseen Christ* is the *key* to all their characters. By faith they lived and walked and stood and overcame.

Would anyone live the life of a Christian soldier? Let him pray for faith. It is the gift of God and a gift which those who ask shall never ask for in vain. You must *believe* before you *fight*. If men do nothing in religion, it is because they do not believe. Faith is the first step towards heaven.

Would anyone fight the fight of a Christian soldier successfully and prosperously? Let him pray for a continual increase of faith. Let him abide in Christ, get closer to Christ, tighten his hold on Christ every day that he lives. Let his daily prayer be that of the disciples: 'Lord, increase my faith' (see Luke 17:5). Watch jealously over your faith, if you have any. It is the citadel of the Christian character, on which the safety of the whole fortress depends. It is the point which Satan loves to assail. All lies at his mercy if faith is overthrown. Here, if we love life, we must especially stand on our guard.

3. True Christianity is a *good* fight

'Good' is a curious word to apply to any warfare. All worldly war is more or less evil. No doubt it is an absolute necessity in many cases – to procure the liberty of nations, to prevent the weak from being trampled down by the strong – but still, war is an evil. It entails a dreadful amount of bloodshed and suffering. It hurries into eternity myriads who are completely unprepared for their change. It calls forth the worst passions of man. It causes enormous waste and destruction of property. It fills peaceful homes with mourning widows and orphans. It spreads poverty, taxation and national distress far and wide. It disarranges all the order of society. It interrupts the work of the gospel and the growth of Christian missions. In short, war is an immense and incalculable evil, and every praying man should cry night and day, 'Give peace in our times.'

And yet there is one warfare which is emphatically 'good' and one fight in which there is no evil. That warfare is the *Christian* warfare. That fight is the fight of the *soul*.

Now, what are the reasons why the Christian fight is a 'good fight'?

What are the points in which his warfare is superior to the warfare of this world? I want my readers to know that there is abundant encouragement, if they will only begin the battle. The Scripture does not call the Christian fight a 'good' fight without reason and cause. Let me try to show what I mean.

a) The Christian's fight is good, because fought under the best of *generals*. The Leader and Commander of all believers is our divine Saviour, the Lord Jesus Christ – a Saviour of ...

perfect wisdom,

infinite love and

almighty power!

The Captain of our salvation never fails to lead His soldiers to victory. He never makes any useless movements, never errs in judgement, never commits any mistake. His eye is on all His followers, from the greatest of them even to the least. The humblest servant in His army is not forgotten. The weakest and most sickly is cared for, remembered and kept unto salvation. The souls whom He has purchased and redeemed with His own blood are far too precious to be wasted and thrown away. Surely this is good!

b) The Christian's fight is good, because fought with the best of *helps*. As weak as each believer is in himself, the Holy Spirit dwells in him, and his body is a temple of the Holy Spirit ...

chosen by God the Father,

washed in the blood of the Son,

renewed by the Spirit –

he does not go to warfare at his own charges, and is never alone.

God the *Holy Spirit* daily teaches, leads, guides and directs him.

God the *Father* guards him by His almighty power.

God the *Son* intercedes for him every moment, like Moses on the mount, while he is fighting in the valley below.

A three-fold cord like this can never be broken! His daily provisions and supplies never fail. His bread and his water are sure. As weak as he seems in himself, like a worm, he is strong in the Lord to do great exploits. Surely this is good!

c) The Christian fight is a good fight, because fought with the best of *promises*. To every believer belong exceeding great and precious promises, all 'yes' and 'amen' in Christ; promises sure to be fulfilled because made by One who cannot lie and who has *power* as well as *will* to keep His word. '... sin shall no longer be your master'; 'The God of peace will soon crush Satan under your feet'; '... he who began a good work in you will carry it on to completion until the day of Christ Jesus'; 'When you pass through the waters, I will be with you; and when you pass through the rivers, they will not sweep over you'; 'My sheep ... shall never perish; no one will snatch them out of my hand'; '... whoever comes to me I will never drive away'; 'Never will I leave you; never will I forsake you'; 'I am convinced that neither death nor life ... neither the present nor the future ... will be able to separate us from the love of God that is in Christ Jesus our Lord' (Rom. 6:14; 16:20; Phil. 1:6; Isa. 43:2; John 10:27,28; 6:37; Heb. 13:5; Rom. 8:38,39).

Words like these are worth their weight in gold! Who does not know that promises of coming aid have cheered the defenders of besieged cities, like Lucknow, and raised them above their natural strength? Have we never heard that the promise of 'help before night' had much to say to the mighty victory of Waterloo? Yet all such promises are as nothing compared to the rich treasure of believers – the eternal promises of God. Surely this is good!

d) The Christian's fight is a good fight, because fought with the best of *outcomes* and results. No doubt it is a war in which there are tremendous struggles, agonizing conflicts, wounds, bruises, watchings, fastings and fatigue. But still, all believers, without exception, are 'more than conquerors through him who loved us' (Rom. 8:37). No soldiers of Christ are ever *lost, missing* or left *dead* on the battlefield. No mourning will ever need to be put on, and no tears to be shed, for either private or officer in the army of Christ. The muster roll, when the last evening comes, will be found precisely the same that it was in the morning.

The English Guards marched out of London to the Crimean campaign a magnificent body of men – but many of the gallant fellows laid their bones in a foreign grave and never saw London again. Far different shall be the arrival of the Christian army in the 'city with foundations, whose architect and builder is God' (Heb. 11:10). Not one shall be found lacking. The words of our great Captain shall be found true: 'I have not lost one of those you gave me' (John 18:9). Surely this is good!

e) The Christian's fight is good, because it does good to the *soul* of him that fights it. All other wars have a bad, lowering and demoralizing tendency. They call forth the *worst passions* of the human mind. They harden the conscience and sap the foundations of religion and morality. The Christian warfare alone tends to call forth the best things that are left in man.

It promotes *humility* and *charity*,

it lessens *selfishness* and *worldliness*,

it induces men to set their affections on things above.

The old, the sick, the dying are never known to repent of fighting Christ's battles against sin, the world and the devil. Their only regret is that they did not begin to serve Christ long before. The experience of that eminent saint, Philip Henry, does not stand alone. In his last days he said to his family, 'I take you all to record that a life spent in the service of Christ, is the happiest life that a man can spend upon earth.' Surely this is good!

f) The Christian's fight is a good fight, because it does good to the *world*. All other wars have a devastating, ravaging and injurious effect. The march of an army through a land is a dreadful scourge to the inhabitants. Wherever it goes it impoverishes, wastes and does harm. Injury to people, property, feelings and morals invariably accompanies it.

Far different are the effects produced by Christian soldiers. Wherever they live, they are a blessing. They raise the standard of religion and morality. They invariably check the progress of drunkenness, profligacy and dishonesty. Even their enemies are obliged to respect them. Go where you please, you will rarely find that barracks and garrisons do good to the neighbourhood. But go where you please, you will find that the presence of a few true Christians is a blessing. Surely this is good!

g) Finally, the Christian's fight is good, because it ends in a glorious *reward* for all who fight it. Who can tell the wages that Christ will pay to all His faithful people? Who can estimate the good things that our divine Captain has laid up for those who confess Him before men? A grateful country can give to her successful warriors medals, pensions, peerages, honours and titles. But it can give nothing that will last and endure forever, nothing that can be carried beyond the grave. Palaces can only be enjoyed for a few years. The bravest generals and soldiers must go down one day before the king of terrors. Better, far better, is the position of him who fights under Christ's banner, against sin, the world and the devil. He may get little praise of man while he lives, and go down to the grave with little honour; but he will have that which is far better, because far more enduring. He will have an unfading crown of glory (see 1 Pet. 5:4). Surely this is good!

Let us settle it in our minds that the Christian fight is a good fight – really good, truly good, emphatically good. We see only part of it yet.

We see the *struggle* – but not the end;

we see the *battle* – but not the reward;

we see the *cross* – but not the crown.

We see a few humble, broken-spirited, penitent, praying people enduring hardships and despised by the world – but we see not ...

the hand of God over them,

the face of God smiling on them,

the kingdom of glory prepared for them.

These things are yet to be revealed. Let us not judge by

appearances. There are more good things about the Christian warfare than we presently see.

To conclude

And now let me conclude my whole subject with a few words of *practical application*. Our lot is cast in times when the world seems thinking of little else but battles and fighting. The iron is entering into the soul of more than one nation, and the mirth of many a fair district is clean gone. Surely in times like these a minister may fairly call on men to remember their spiritual warfare. Let me say a few parting words about *the great fight of the soul*.

1. It may be you are struggling hard for the rewards of this world. Perhaps you are straining every nerve to obtain money or place or power or pleasure. If that be your case, take care. You are sowing a crop of bitter disappointment. Unless you mind what you are about, your latter end will be to lie down in sorrow.

Thousands have trodden the path you are pursuing and have awoke too late to find it end in misery and eternal ruin. They have fought hard for wealth and honour and office and promotion and turned their backs on God and Christ and heaven and the world to come. And what has their end been? Often, far too often, they have found out that *their whole life has been a grand mistake*. They have tasted by bitter experience the feelings of the dying statesman who cried aloud in his last hours, 'The battle is fought; the battle is fought; but the victory is not won!'

For your own happiness' sake, resolve this day to join the Lord's side. Shake off your past carelessness and unbelief. Come out from the ways of a thoughtless, unreasoning world. Take up the cross, and become a good soldier of Christ. 'Fight the good fight of the faith' that you may be happy as well as safe.

Think what the people of this world will often do for liberty, without any religious principle. Remember how Greeks and Romans and Swiss have endured the loss of all things, and even life itself, rather than bend their necks to a foreign yoke. Let their example provoke you to emulation. If men can do so much for a corruptible crown, how much more should you do for one which is incorruptible? Awake to a sense of the misery of being a slave. For life and happiness and liberty – arise and fight!

Fear not to begin and enlist under Christ's banner. The great Captain of your salvation rejects none that come to Him. Like David in the cave of Adullam, He is ready to receive all who apply to Him, however unworthy they may feel themselves. None who repent and believe are too bad to be enrolled in the ranks of Christ's army. All who come to Him by faith are admitted, clothed, armed, trained and finally led on to complete victory. Fear not to begin this very day. There is yet room for you.

Fear not to go on fighting, if you once enlist. The more thorough and wholehearted you are as a soldier, the more comfortable will you find your warfare. No doubt you will often meet with trouble, fatigue and hard fighting before your warfare is accomplished. But let none of these things move you. Greater is He who is for you than all those who are against you. Everlasting liberty or everlasting captivity are the alternatives before you. Choose liberty, and fight to the last!

2. It may be you know something of the Christian warfare and are a tried and proved soldier already. If that be your case, accept a parting word of advice and encouragement from a fellow soldier. Let me speak to myself as well as to you. Let us stir up our minds by way of remembrance. There are some things which we cannot remember too well.

Let us remember that if we would fight successfully, we must put on the whole armour of God, and never lay it aside until we die. Not a single piece of the armour can be dispensed with.

The belt of truth,

the breastplate of righteousness,

the shield of faith,

the sword of the Spirit,

the helmet of hope –

each and all are needful. Not a single day can we dispense with any part of this armour. Well says an old veteran in Christ's army, who died 200 years ago, 'In heaven we shall appear, not in armour, but in robes of glory. But here these are to be worn night and day; we must walk, work, and sleep in them, or else we are not true soldiers of Christ.'

Let us remember the solemn words of an inspired warrior, who went to his rest 1,800 years ago: 'No one serving as a soldier gets entangled in civilian affairs, but rather tries to please his commanding officer' (2 Tim. 2:4). May we never forget that saying!

Let us remember that some have seemed good soldiers for a little season, and talked loudly of what they would do – and yet turned back disgracefully in the day of battle.

Let us never forget Balaam and Judas and Demas and Lot's wife.

Whatever we are, and however weak, let us be real, genuine, true and sincere.

Let us remember that the eye of our loving Saviour is upon us morning, noon and night. He will never allow us to be tempted above what we are able to bear. He can be touched with the feeling of our infirmities, for He suffered Himself, being tempted. He knows what battles and conflicts are, for He Himself was assaulted by the prince of this world. Having such a High Priest, Jesus the Son of God, 'let us hold firmly to the faith we profess' (Heb. 4:14).

Let us remember that thousands of soldiers before us have fought the same battle that we are fighting, and come off more than conquerors through Him who loved them. They overcame by the blood of the Lamb – and so also may we. Christ's *arm* is quite as strong as ever, and Christ's *heart* is just as loving as ever. He who saved men and women before us is One who never changes. He is 'able to save completely those who come to God through him'. Then let us cast doubts and fears away. Let us follow those 'who through faith and patience inherit what has been promised' and are waiting for us to join them (Heb. 7:25; 6:12).

Finally, let us remember that *the time is short*, and the coming of the Lord draws near. A few more battles – and then the last trumpet shall sound, and the Prince of Peace shall come to reign on a renewed earth. A few more struggles and conflicts, and then we shall bid an eternal goodbye to warfare and to sin, to sorrow and to death. Then let us fight on to the last and never surrender. Thus says the Captain of our salvation: 'Those who are victorious will inherit all this, and I will be their God and they will be my children' (Rev. 21:7).

Let me conclude all with the words of John Bunyan in one of the most beautiful parts of *The Pilgrim's Progress*. He is describing the end of one of his best and holiest pilgrims:

> After this it was noised abroad that Mr *Valiant-for-Truth* was taken with a summons ... When he understood it, he called for his friends, and told them of it. Then said he, 'I am going to my father's, and though with great difficulty I am got hither, yet now I do not repent me of all the trouble I have been at to arrive where I am. My sword, I give to him that shall succeed me in my pilgrimage, and my courage and skill, to him that can get it. My marks and scars I carry with me, to be a witness for me that I have fought his battles who will now be my Rewarder.' When the day that he must go hence was come many accompanied him to the River side, into which, as he went, he said, '*Death, where is thy sting?*' And as he went down deeper, he said, '*Grave where is thy victory?*' So he passed over, and the trumpets sounded for him on the other side.

May our end be like this! May we never forget that without fighting, there can be no holiness while we live, and no crown of glory when we die!

5

The Cost

'Suppose one of you wants to build a tower. Won't you first sit down and estimate the cost ...?'

(Luke 14:28)

The text which heads this page is one of great importance. Few are the people who are not often obliged to ask themselves, 'What does it cost?'

In buying property, in building houses, in furnishing rooms, in forming plans, in changing dwellings, in educating children, it is wise and prudent to look forward and consider the cost. Many would save themselves much sorrow and trouble if they would only remember the question: 'What does it cost?'

But there is one subject on which it is especially important to count the cost. That subject is the salvation of our souls. What does it cost to be a true Christian? What does it cost to be a really holy man? This, after all, is the grand question. For lack of thought about this, thousands, after seeming to begin well, turn away from the road to heaven, and are lost forever in hell.

We are living in unusual times. Events are hurrying on with singular rapidity. We never know 'what a day may bring forth'; how much less do we know what may happen in a year! We live in a day of great religious profession. Scores of professing Christians in every part of the land are expressing a desire for more holiness and a higher degree of spiritual life. Yet nothing is more common than to see people receiving the Word with joy, and then after two or three years, falling away and going back to their sins. *They had not considered what it costs to be a really consistent believer and holy Christian.* Surely these are times when we ought often to sit down and count the cost and to consider the state of our souls. We must mind what we are about. If we *desire* to be truly holy, it is a good sign. We may thank God for putting the desire into our hearts. But still the *cost* ought to be counted. No doubt Christ's way to eternal life is a way of pleasantness. But it is folly to shut our eyes to the fact that His way is *narrow* and the *cross* comes before the crown.

The cost of being a true Christian

Let there be no mistake about my meaning. I am not examining what it costs to save a Christian's soul. I know well that it costs nothing less than the blood of the Son of God to provide an atonement, and to redeem man from hell. The price paid for our redemption was nothing less than the death of Jesus Christ on Calvary. We 'were bought at a price'; Christ 'gave himself as a ransom for all people' (1 Cor. 6:20; 1 Tim. 2:6). But all this is wide of the question.

The point I want to consider is another one altogether. It is what a man must be ready to give up, if he wishes to be saved. It is the amount of sacrifice a man must submit to if he intends to serve Christ. It is in this sense that I raise the question: 'What does it cost?' And I believe firmly that it is a most important one.

I grant freely that it costs little to be a mere outward Christian. A man has only got to attend a place of worship twice on Sunday, and to be tolerably moral during the week, and he has gone as far as thousands around him ever go in religion. All this is cheap and easy work – it entails no self-denial or self-sacrifice. If this is saving Christianity and will take us to heaven when we die, we must alter the description of the way of life, and write, 'Wide is the gate and broad is the way that leads to heaven'!

But it does cost something to be a real Christian, according to the standard of the Bible. There are ...

enemies to be overcome,

battles to be fought,

sacrifices to be made,

an Egypt to be forsaken,

a wilderness to be passed through,

a cross to be carried,

a race to be run.

Conversion is not putting a man in a soft armchair and taking him pleasantly to heaven. It is the beginning of a mighty conflict, in which it costs much to win the victory. Hence arises the unspeakable importance of 'counting the cost'.

Let me try to show precisely and particularly what it costs to be a true Christian. Let us suppose that a man is disposed to take service with Christ and feels drawn and inclined to follow Him. Let us suppose that some affliction or some sudden death or an awakening sermon has stirred his conscience and made him feel the value of his soul and desire to be a true Christian. No doubt there is everything to encourage him. His sins may be freely forgiven, however many and great. His heart may be completely changed, however cold and hard. Christ and the Holy Spirit, mercy and grace are all ready for him. But still, he should count the cost. Let us see particularly, one by one, the things that his religion will cost him.

1. True Christianity will cost one his *self-righteousness*. He must cast away all pride and high thoughts and conceit of his own goodness. He must be content to go to heaven as a poor sinner saved only by free grace, and owing all to the merit and righteousness of another. He must really feel that he has 'erred and gone astray like a lost sheep' that he has 'left undone the things he ought to have done, and that there is no strength in him'. He must be willing to give up all trust in his own morality, respectability, praying, Bible-reading, church-going and sacrament receiving, and to trust in nothing but Jesus Christ.

2. True Christianity will cost a man his *sins*. He must be willing to give up every habit and practice which is wrong in God's sight. He must set his face against it, quarrel with it, break off from it, fight with it, crucify it and labour to keep it under control, whatever the world around him may say or think. He must do this honestly and fairly. There must be no secret truce with any special sin which he loves. He must count all sins as his deadly enemies, and hate every false way. Whether little or great, whether open or secret – all his sins must be thoroughly renounced. They may struggle hard with him every day, and sometimes almost get the mastery over him. But he must never give way to them. He must keep up a perpetual war with his sins. It is written, 'Rid yourselves of all the offences you have committed'; '... renounce your sins ... and your wickedness'; '... stop doing wrong' (Ezek. 18:31; Dan. 4:27; Isa. 1:16).

This sounds hard. I do not wonder. Our sins are often as dear to us as our children! We love them, hug them, cleave to them and delight in them! To part with them is as hard as cutting off a right hand or plucking out a right eye. But it must be done. The parting must come. 'Though evil is sweet in [the sinner's] mouth and he hides it under his tongue, though he cannot bear to let it go', yet it must be given up, if he wishes to be saved (Job 20:12,13). He and sin must quarrel, if he and God are to be friends. Christ is willing to receive any *sinners*. But He will not receive them if they will stick to their sins.

3. Also, Christianity will cost a man his love of *ease*. He must take pains and trouble, if he means to run a successful race towards heaven. He must daily watch and stand on his guard, like a soldier on enemy's ground. He must take heed to his behaviour every hour of the day, in every company and in every place, in public as well as in private, among strangers as well as at home. He must be careful over his time, his tongue, his temper, his thoughts, his imagination, his motives, his conduct in every relation of life. He must be diligent about his prayers, his Bible-reading and his use of Sundays, with all their means of grace. In attending to these things, he may come far short of perfection; but there is none of them who he can safely neglect. 'A sluggard's appetite is never filled, but the desires of the diligent are fully satisfied' (Prov. 13:4).

This also sounds hard. There is nothing we naturally dislike so much as 'trouble' about our religion. We hate trouble. We secretly wish we could have a vicarious Christianity, and could be good by proxy, and have everything done for us. Anything that requires exertion and labour is entirely against the grain of our hearts. But the soul can have 'no gains without pains'.

4. Lastly, true Christianity will cost a man the favour of the world. He must be content to be thought poorly of by man – if he pleases God. He must count it no strange thing to be mocked, ridiculed, slandered, persecuted and even hated. He must not be surprised to find that his opinions and practices are despised and held up to scorn. He must submit to be thought by many a fool, an enthusiast and a fanatic – to have his words perverted and his actions misrepresented. In fact, he must not marvel if some call him *mad*. The Master says, 'Remember what I told you: "A servant is not greater than his master. If they persecuted me, they will persecute you also"' (John 15:20).

I dare say this also sounds hard. We naturally dislike unjust dealing and false charges, and think it very hard to be accused without cause. We would not be flesh and blood if we did not wish to have the good opinion of our neighbours. It is always unpleasant to be spoken against and forsaken and lied about – and to stand alone. But there is no help for it. The cup which our Master drank must be drunk by His disciples. They must be 'despised and rejected by mankind' (Isa. 53:3). Let us set down that item last in our account. To be a Christian, it will cost a man the favour of the world.

Considering the weight of this great cost, bold indeed must that man be who would dare to say that we may keep our self-righteousness, our sins, our laziness and our love of the world – and yet be saved!

Moreover, I grant it costs much to be a true Christian. But what sane man or woman can doubt that it is *worth any cost* to have the soul saved? When the ship is in danger of sinking, the crew think nothing of casting overboard the precious cargo. When a limb is mortified, a man will submit to any severe operation, and even to amputation – to save life. Surely a Christian should be willing to give up anything which stands between him and heaven. *A religion which costs nothing is worth nothing! A cheap, easy Christianity, without a cross, will prove in the end a useless Christianity, without a crown!*

The importance of counting the cost

I might easily settle this question by laying down the principle that no duty enjoined by Christ can ever be neglected without damage. I might show how many shut their eyes throughout life to the nature of saving religion and refuse to consider what it really costs to be a Christian. I might describe how at last, when life is ebbing away, they wake up and make a few spasmodic efforts to turn to God. I might tell you how they find, to their amazement, that repentance and conversion are no such easy matters as they had supposed, and that it costs 'a great sum' to be a true Christian. They discover that habits of pride, and sinful indulgence, and love of ease, and worldliness are not so easily laid aside as they had dreamed. And so, after a faint struggle, they give up in despair, and leave the world hopeless, graceless and unfit to meet God! They had *flattered* themselves all their days that religion would be easy work when they once took it up seriously. But they open their eyes too late, and discover for the first time that they are *ruined* because they never counted the cost.

But there is a certain group of people to whom especially I wish to address myself in handling this part of my subject. It is a large class, an increasing class and a class which in these days is in peculiar danger. Let me in a few plain words try to describe this class. It deserves our best attention.

The people I speak of are not thoughtless about religion; they think a good deal about it. They are not ignorant of religion; they know the outlines of it pretty well. But their great defect is that they are not 'rooted and grounded' in their faith. Too often they have picked up their knowledge second-hand, from being in religious families, or from being trained in religious ways – but have never worked it out by their own inward experience. Too often they have hastily taken up a profession of religion under the pressure of circumstances, from sentimental feelings, from emotional excitement or from a vague desire to do like others around them, but without any solid work of grace in their hearts. People like these are in a position of immense danger. They are precisely those, if Bible examples are worth anything, who need to be exhorted to *count the cost*.

For lack of counting the cost, myriads of the children of Israel perished miserably in the wilderness between Egypt and Canaan. They left Egypt full of zeal and fervour as if nothing could stop them. But when they found dangers and difficulties in the way, their courage soon cooled down. They had never reckoned on trouble. They had thought the Promised Land would be before them in a few days. And so when enemies, privations, hunger and thirst began to try them, they murmured against Moses and God and would gladly have gone back to Egypt. In a word, they had not counted the cost – and so lost everything and died in their sins!

For lack of counting the cost, many of our Lord Jesus Christ's hearers went back after a time and 'no longer followed him' (John 6:66). When they first saw His miracles and heard His preaching, they thought 'the kingdom of God was going to appear at once' (Luke 19:11). They cast in their lot with His apostles and followed Him without thinking of the consequences. But when they found that there were hard doctrines to be believed, and hard work to be done, and hard treatment to be borne, their faith gave way entirely and proved to be nothing at all. In a word, they had not counted the cost, and so made shipwreck of their profession.

For lack of counting the cost, King Herod returned to his old sins and destroyed his soul. He liked to hear John the Baptist preach. He observed and honoured him as a just and holy man. He even 'did many things' (Mark 6:20, KJV) which were right and good. But when he found that he must give up his darling Herodias, his religion entirely broke down. He had not reckoned on this. He had not counted the cost.

For lack of counting the cost, Demas forsook the company of Paul, forsook the gospel, forsook Christ, forsook heaven. For a long time he journeyed with the great apostle of the Gentiles, and was actually one of his 'fellow workers' (Phlm. 24). But when he found he could not have the friendship of this world as well as the friendship of God, he gave up his Christianity and cleaved to the world. 'Demas ... has deserted me,' says Paul, 'because he loved this world' (2 Tim. 4:10). He had not 'counted the cost'.

For lack of counting the cost, the hearers of powerful evangelical preachers often come to miserable ends. They are stirred and excited into professing what they have not really experienced. They receive the Word with a 'joy' so extravagant that it almost startles old Christians. They run for a time with such zeal and fervour that they seem likely to outstrip all others. They talk and work for spiritual objects with such enthusiasm that they make older believers feel ashamed. But when the novelty and freshness of their feelings is gone, a change comes over them. They prove to have been nothing more than stony ground hearers. The description the great Master gives in the parable of the sower is exactly exemplified: 'But since they have no root, they last only a short time. When trouble or persecution comes because of the word, they quickly fall away' (Matt. 13:21). Little by little their zeal melts away and their love becomes cold. By and by their seats are empty in the assembly of God's people, and they are heard of no more among Christians. And why? They had never counted the cost.

For lack of counting the cost, hundreds of professed converts, under religious revivals, go back to the world after a time and bring disgrace on religion. They begin with a sadly mistaken notion of what is true Christianity. They imagine it consists in nothing more than a so-called 'coming to Christ' and having strong inward feelings of joy and peace. And so when they find, after a time, that there is a *cross* to be carried, that our *hearts* are deceitful, and that there is a *busy devil* always near us, they cool down in disgust and return to their old sins. And why? Because they had really never known what Bible Christianity is. They had never learned that we must count the cost.

For lack of counting the cost, the children of religious parents often turn out badly and bring disgrace on Christianity. Familiar from their earliest years with the form and theory of the gospel, taught even from infancy to repeat great leading texts, accustomed every week to be instructed in the gospel, or to instruct others in Sunday schools, they often grow up professing a religion without knowing why, or without ever having thought seriously about it. And then when the realities of grown-up life begin to press upon them, they often astound everyone by dropping all their religion and plunging right into the world! And why? They had never thoroughly understood the *sacrifices* which Christianity entails. They had never been taught to count the cost.

These are solemn and painful truths. But they are truths. They all help to show the immense importance of the subject I am now considering. They all point out the absolute necessity of pressing the subject of this message on all who profess a desire for holiness and of crying aloud in all the churches, 'Count the cost.'

I am bold to say that it would be well if the duty of counting the cost were more frequently taught than it is. *Impatient hurry* is the order of the day with many religionists. Instantaneous conversions and immediate sensible peace are the only results they seem to care for from the gospel. Compared with these, all other things are thrown into the shade. To produce them is the grand end and object, apparently, of all their labours. I say without hesitation that such a naked, one-sided mode of teaching Christianity is mischievous in the extreme!

Let no one mistake my meaning. I thoroughly approve of offering men a full, free, present, immediate salvation in Christ Jesus. I thoroughly approve of urging on man the possibility and the duty of immediate instantaneous conversion. In these matters I give place to no one. But I do say that these truths ought not to be set before men nakedly, singly and alone. They ought to be told *honestly* what it is they are taking up, if they profess a desire to come out from the world and serve Christ. They ought not to be pressed into the ranks of Christ's army, without being told what the warfare entails. In a word, they should be told honestly to count the cost.

Does anyone ask what our Lord Jesus Christ's practice was in this matter? Let him read what Luke records. He tells us that on a certain occasion, 'Large crowds were travelling with Jesus, and turning to them he said: "If anyone comes to me and does not hate father and mother, wife and children, brothers and sisters – yes, even their own life – such a person cannot be my disciple. And whoever does not carry their cross and follow me cannot be my disciple"' (Luke 14:25–27). I must plainly say that I cannot reconcile this passage with the proceedings of many modern religious teachers. And yet, to my mind, the doctrine of it is as clear as the sun at noonday. It shows us that *we ought not to hurry men into professing discipleship, without warning them plainly to count the cost.*

Does anyone ask what the practice of the eminent and best preachers of the gospel has been in days gone by? I am bold to say that they have all with one mouth borne testimony to the wisdom of our Lord's dealing with the multitudes to which I have just referred. Luther and Latimer and Baxter and Wesley and Whitefield and Berridge and Rowland Hill were all keenly alive to the deceitfulness of man's heart. They knew full well that ...

all is not gold that glitters,

that conviction is not conversion,

that feeling is not faith,

that sentiment is not grace,

that all blossoms do not come to fruit.

'Be not deceived,' was their constant cry. 'Consider well what you do. Do not run before you are called. Count the cost.'

If we desire to do good, let us never be ashamed of walking in the steps of our Lord Jesus Christ. Press others to consider their ways. Compel them with holy violence to come in, to lay down their arms and to yield themselves to God. Offer them salvation, ready, free, full, immediate salvation. Press Christ and all His benefits on their acceptance. But in all your work tell the truth, and the whole truth. Be ashamed to use the vulgar arts of a recruiting sergeant. Do not speak only of the uniform, the pay and the glory; speak also of the enemies, the battle, the armour, the watching, the marching and the drill. Do not present only one side of Christianity. Do not keep back the cross of self-denial that must be carried, when you speak of the cross on which Christ died for our redemption. Explain fully what Christianity entails. *Entreat men to repent and come to Christ – but bid them at the same time to count the cost!*

Some hints that may help men to rightly count the cost

Sorry indeed would I be if I did not say something on this branch of my subject. I have no wish to discourage anyone or to keep anyone back from Christ's service. It is my heart's desire to encourage everyone to go forward and take up the cross. Let us count the cost by all means, and count it carefully. But let us remember that if we count rightly and look on all sides, there is nothing that need make us afraid.

Let me mention some things which should always enter into our calculations in counting the cost of true Christianity. Set down honestly and fairly what you will have to give up and go through, if you become Christ's disciple. Leave nothing out. Put it all down. But then set down side by side the following sums which I am going to give you. Do this fairly and correctly, and I am not afraid for the result.

a) Count up and compare the *profit and the loss* – if you are a true-hearted and holy Christian. You may possibly lose something in this world, but you will gain the salvation of your immortal soul. It is written: 'What good is it for someone to gain the whole world, yet forfeit their soul?' (Mark 8:36).

b) Count up and compare the *praise and the blame* – if you are a true-hearted and holy Christian. You may possibly be blamed by man – but you will have the praise of God the Father, God the Son and God the Holy Spirit. Your blame will come from the lips of a few erring, blind, fallible men and women. Your praise will come from the King of kings and Judge of all the earth. It is only those whom He blesses who are really blessed. It is written: '*Blessed* are you when people insult you, persecute you and falsely say all kinds of evil against you because of me. Rejoice and be glad, because great is your reward in heaven' (Matt. 5:11,12, italics mine).

c) Count up and compare *the friends and the enemies* – if you are a true-hearted and holy Christian. On the one side of you is the enmity of the devil and the wicked. On the other, you have the favour and friendship of the Lord Jesus Christ. Your enemies, at most, can only bruise your heel. They may rage loudly and compass sea and land to work your ruin – but they cannot destroy you. Your Friend is able to save to the uttermost all those who come unto God by Him. None shall ever pluck His sheep out of His hand. It is written: '... do not be afraid of those who kill the body and after that can do no more. But I will show you whom you should fear: fear him who, after your body has been killed, has authority to throw you into hell. Yes, I tell you, fear him' (Luke 12:4,5).

d) Count up and compare *the life that now is and the life to come* – if you are a true-hearted and holy Christian. The time present, no doubt, is not a time of ease. It is a time of watching and praying, fighting and struggling, believing and working. But it is only for a few years. The time future is the season of rest and refreshing. Sin shall be cast out. Satan shall be bound. And, best of all, it shall be a rest *forever*. It is written: 'For our light and momentary troubles are achieving for us an eternal glory that far outweighs them all. So we fix our eyes not on what is seen, but on what is unseen, since what is seen is temporary, but what is unseen is eternal' (2 Cor. 4:17,18).

e) Count up and compare the *pleasures of sin and the happiness of God's service* – if you are a true-hearted and holy Christian. The pleasures that the worldly man gets by his ways are hollow, unreal and unsatisfying. They are like the fire of thorns, flashing and crackling for a few minutes, and then quenched forever. The happiness that Christ gives to His people is something solid, lasting and substantial. It is not dependent on health or circumstances. It never leaves a man, even in death. It ends in an unfading crown of glory! It is written: '... the joy of the godless lasts but a moment'; 'Like the crackling of thorns under the pot, so is the laughter of fools' (Job 20:5; Eccl. 7:6). But it is also written: 'Peace I leave with you; my peace I give you. I do not give to you as the world gives. Do not let your hearts be troubled and do not be afraid' (John 14:27).

f) Count up and compare the trouble that true Christianity entails – and the troubles that are in store for the wicked beyond the grave. Grant for a moment that Bible-reading and praying and repenting and believing and holy living require pains and self-denial. It is all nothing compared to that wrath to come which is stored up for the impenitent and unbelieving! A single day in hell will be worse than a whole life spent in carrying the cross. The 'worm that never dies, and the fire that is not quenched' (see Mark 9:43–48) are things which it passes man's power to fully conceive or describe. It is written: 'Son, remember that in your lifetime you received your good things, while Lazarus received bad things, but now he is comforted here and you are in agony' (Luke 16:25).

g) Count up and compare the number of those who turn from sin and the world and serve Christ – and the number of those who forsake Christ and return to the world. On the one side you will find thousands; on the other you will find none. Multitudes are every year turning out of the broad way and entering the narrow way.

None who really enter the narrow way grow tired of it and return to the broad way. The footsteps in the downward road are often to be seen turning out of it. The footsteps in the road to heaven are all *one way*. It is written: '... the way of the wicked is like deep darkness'; '... the way of the unfaithful leads to their destruction' (Prov. 4:19; 13:15). But it is also written: 'The path of the righteous is like the morning sun, shining ever brighter till the full light of day' (Prov. 4:18).

Such *sums* as these, no doubt, are often not done correctly. Many, I am well aware, are ever 'halting between two opinions'. They cannot make up their minds that it is worthwhile to serve Christ.

The losses – and the gains,

the advantages – and the disadvantages,

the sorrows – and the joys,

the helps – and the hindrances –

appear to them so nearly balanced that they cannot decide for God. They cannot do this great sum correctly. They cannot make the result so clear as it ought to be. They do not *count right*!

But *why* do they err so greatly? They lack *faith*. Paul advises us on how to come to a right conclusion about our souls in Hebrews 11, revealing a powerful principle that operates in the business of counting the cost. It is the same principle Noah understood, and that I will now make clear.

How was it that *Noah* persevered in building the ark? He stood alone amid a world of sinners and unbelievers. He had to endure scorn, ridicule and mockery. What was it that nerved his arm, and made him patiently work on and face it all? It was *faith*. He believed in a wrath to come. He believed that there was no safety excepting in the ark that he was preparing. Believing, he held the world's opinion very cheap. He counted the cost by faith, and had no doubt that to build the ark was gain.

How was it that *Moses* forsook the pleasures of Pharaoh's house and refused to be called the son of Pharaoh's daughter? How was it that he cast in his lot with a despised people like the Hebrews, and risked everything in this world in carrying out the great work of their deliverance from bondage? To the eye of *sense* he was losing everything and gaining nothing. What was it that moved him? It was faith. He believed that he would be 'richly rewarded' for his 'confidence' (Heb. 10:35) and that this was far better than all the honours of Egypt. He counted the cost by faith, 'because he saw him who is invisible' (Heb. 11:27), and was persuaded that to forsake Egypt and go forth into the wilderness was gain.

How was it that *Saul* the Pharisee could ever make up his mind to become a Christian? The cost and sacrifices of the change were fearfully great. He gave up all his brilliant prospects among his own people. He brought on himself, instead of man's favour, man's hatred, man's enmity and man's persecution, even unto death. What was it that enabled him to face it all? It was faith. He believed that Jesus, who met him on the way to Damascus, could give him a hundred-fold more than he gave up, and in the world to come, everlasting life. By faith he *counted the cost* and saw clearly on which side the balance lay. He believed firmly that to carry the cross of Christ was gain.

Let us mark well these things. That faith which made Noah, Moses and Paul do what they did, that faith is the great secret of coming to a right conclusion about our souls. That same faith must be our helper and ready-reckoner when we sit down to count the cost of being a true Christian. That same faith is to be had for the asking. '... he gives us more grace' (Jas. 4:6). Armed with that faith – we shall set things down at their true value. Filled with that faith – we shall neither add to the cross, nor subtract from the crown. Our conclusions will be all correct. Our *sum total* will be without error.

1. Now, let us make the serious inquiry: *What does your Christianity cost you?* Very likely it costs you nothing. Very probably it neither costs you trouble, nor time, nor thought, nor care, nor pains, nor reading, nor praying, nor self-denial, nor conflict, nor working, nor labour of any kind. Now mark carefully what I say. Such a religion as this will never save your soul. It will never give you peace while you live nor hope while you die. It will not support you in the day of affliction nor cheer you in the hour of death. *A religion which costs nothing is worth nothing!* Awake before it is too late. Awake and repent. Awake and be converted. Awake and believe. Awake and pray. Rest not until you can give a satisfactory answer to my question: 'What does it cost?'

2. Think, if you want stirring motives for serving God, what it cost to provide a salvation for your soul. Think how the Son of God left heaven and became man, suffered on the cross and lay in the grave, to pay your sin-debt to God, and work out for you a complete redemption. Think of all this, and learn that it is no light matter to possess an immortal soul. It is worthwhile to take some trouble about one's soul.

Ah, lazy man or woman, has it really come to this – that you will miss heaven for lack of trouble? Are you really determined to make shipwreck forever, from mere dislike to exertion? Away with the cowardly, unworthy thought. Arise and play the man. Say to yourself, 'Whatever it may cost, I will, at any rate, strive to enter in at the small gate.' Look at the cross of Christ and take fresh courage. Look forward to death, judgement and eternity, and be in earnest. It may cost much to be a Christian – but you may be sure it pays.

3. If any reader of this message really feels that he has counted the cost and taken up the cross, I bid him persevere and press on. I dare say you often feel your heart faint and are sorely tempted to give up in despair. Your enemies seem so many, your besetting sins so strong, your friends so few, the way so steep and narrow, that you hardly know what to do! But still I say, persevere and press on.

The time is very short!

A few more years of watching and praying,

a few more tossings on the sea of this world,

a few more deaths and changes,

a few more winters and summers –

and all will be over. We shall have fought our last battle, and shall need to fight no more.

The presence and company of Christ will make amends for all we suffer here below. When we see as we have been seen, and look back on the journey of life, we shall wonder at our own faintness of heart. We shall marvel that we made so much of our *cross* and thought so little of our *crown*. We shall marvel that in 'counting the cost' we could ever doubt on which side the balance of profit lay. Let us take courage. We are not far from home. It may cost much to be a true Christian and a consistent holy man – but it pays!

6

Growth in Grace

'... grow in the grace and knowledge of our Lord and Saviour Jesus Christ

(2 Pet. 3:18)

The subject of the text which heads this page is one that ought to be deeply interesting to every true Christian. It naturally raises the questions: 'Do *we* grow in grace?' 'Do we *advance* in our religion?' 'Do we make *progress*?'

To a *mere formal* Christian, I cannot expect the inquiry to seem worth attention. The man who has nothing more than a kind of Sunday religion – whose Christianity is like his Sunday clothes, put on once a week, and then laid aside – such a man cannot, of course, be expected to care about growth in grace. He knows nothing about such matters. They are foolishness to him (1 Cor. 2:14). But to everyone who is in downright earnest about his soul, and hungers and thirsts after spiritual life, the question ought to come home with searching power. Do we make progress in our religion? Do we grow?

The question is one that is always *useful* but especially so at certain seasons. A Saturday night, a communion Sunday, the return of a birthday, the end of a year – all these are seasons that ought to set us thinking and make us look within. Time is fast flying. Life is fast ebbing away. The hour is daily drawing nearer when the *reality* of our Christianity will be tested, and it will be seen whether we have built on 'the rock' or on 'the sand'. Surely it befits us from time to time to examine ourselves and take account of our souls? Do we advance in spiritual things? Do we grow?

The question is one that is of special importance in the present day. Crude and strange opinions are floating in men's minds on some points of doctrine, and among others, on *whether growth in grace is an essential part of true holiness*. By some it is totally *denied*. By others it is *explained away* and pared down to nothing. By thousands it is *misunderstood* and consequently *neglected*. In a day like this, it is useful to look fairly in the face the whole subject of Christian growth.

As we consider this subject, I want to make mention of ...

the *reality* of growth in grace,

the *marks* or signs of growth in grace,

and the *means* of growth in grace.

I do not know you, into whose hands this text may have fallen. But I am not ashamed to ask your best attention to its contents. Believe me, the subject is no mere matter of idle speculation and controversy. It is an eminently practical subject, if any is in religion. It is intimately and inseparably connected with the whole question of sanctification. It is a leading mark of *true* saints – that they *grow*. The spiritual health and prosperity, the spiritual happiness and comfort of every true-hearted and holy Christian are intimately connected with the subject of spiritual growth.

1. The reality of growth in grace

That any professor should deny the reality of Christian growth is at first sight a strange and melancholy thing. But it is fair to remember that man's *understanding* is fallen, no less than his *will*. Disagreements about doctrines are often nothing more than disagreements about the meaning of words. I try to hope that it is so in the present case. I try to believe that when I speak of growth in grace and maintain it, I mean one thing while my brethren who deny it mean quite another. Let me therefore clear the way by explaining what I mean.

When I speak of growth in grace, I do not for a moment mean that a believer's saving interest in Christ can grow. I do not mean that he can grow in safety, acceptance with God or security. I do not mean that he can ever be more justified, more pardoned, more forgiven, more at peace with God than he is the first moment that he believes. I hold firmly that the justification of a believer is a finished, perfect and complete work – and that the weakest saint, though he may not know and feel it, is as completely justified as the strongest.

I hold firmly that our election, calling and standing in Christ admit of no degrees, increase or diminishing. If anyone dreams that by growth in grace I mean growth in justification, he is utterly wide of the mark and utterly mistaken about the whole point I am considering.

I would go to the stake, God helping me, for the glorious truth, that in the matter of justification before God every believer is complete in Christ (Col. 2:10). Nothing can be added to his justification from the moment he believes, and nothing taken away.

When I speak of growth in grace, I only mean increase in the degree, size, strength, vigour and power of the graces which the Holy Spirit plants in a believer's heart. I hold that every one of those graces admits of growth, progress and increase. I hold that repentance, faith, hope, love, humility, zeal, courage and the like may be ...

little or great,

strong or weak,

vigorous or feeble – and

may vary greatly in the same man at different periods of his life.

When I speak of a man growing in grace, I mean simply that ...

his sense of sin is becoming deeper,

his faith is becoming stronger,

his hope is becoming brighter,

his love is becoming more extensive,

his spiritual-mindedness is becoming more marked,

he feels more of the power of godliness in his own heart – and he manifests more of it in his life. He is going on from strength to strength, from faith to faith and from grace to grace. I leave it to others to describe such a man's condition by any words they please. For myself I think the truest and best account of him is this – he is growing in grace.

One principal ground on which I build this doctrine of growth in grace is the plain language of Scripture. If words in the Bible mean anything, there is such a thing as growth, and believers ought to be exhorted to grow. What does *Paul* say? '... your faith is growing more and more' (2 Thess. 1:3); '... we urge you ... to do so more and more' (1 Thess. 4:10); '... growing in the knowledge of God' (Col. 1:10); 'Our hope is that ... your faith continues to grow' (2 Cor. 10:15); 'May the Lord make your love increase' (1 Thess. 3:12); that you 'will grow to become in every respect the mature body of him' (Eph. 4:15); 'And this is my prayer: that your love may abound more and more' (Phil. 1:9); '... we ask you ... to do this more and more. For you know what instructions we gave you by the authority of the Lord Jesus' (1 Thess. 4:1,2). What does *Peter* say? '... crave pure spiritual milk, so that by it you may grow up' (1 Pet. 2:2); '... grow in the grace and knowledge of our Lord and Saviour Jesus Christ' (2 Pet. 3:18). I know not what others think of such texts. To me, they seem to establish the doctrine for which I contend and to be incapable of any other explanation. Growth in grace is taught in the Bible. I might stop here and say no more.

The other ground, however, on which I build the doctrine of growth in grace, is the ground of fact and experience. I ask any honest reader of the New Testament whether he cannot see degrees of grace in the New Testament saints whose histories are recorded, as plainly as the sun at noonday. I ask him whether he cannot see, in the very same people, as great a difference between their faith and knowledge at one time and at another as between the same man's strength when he is an infant and when he is a grown-up man. I ask him whether the Scripture does not distinctly recognize this in the language it uses when it speaks of 'weak' faith and 'strong' faith, and of Christians as 'newborn babies', 'children', 'fathers' and 'young men' (1 Pet. 2:2; 1 John 2:12–14)?

I ask him, above all, whether his own observation of believers nowadays does not bring him to the same conclusion? What true Christian would not confess that there is as much difference between the degree of his own faith and knowledge when he was *first* converted and his *present* attainments as there is between a sapling and a full-grown tree? His graces are the same in principle but they have *grown*. I know not how these facts strike others; to my eyes they seem to prove, most unanswerably, that growth in grace is a real thing.

I feel almost ashamed to dwell so long upon this part of my subject. In fact, if any man means to say that the faith and hope and knowledge and holiness of a newly converted person are as strong as those of an old-established believer and need no increase – it is a waste of time to argue further. No doubt they are ...

as real – but not so strong;

as true – but not so vigorous;

as much seeds of the Spirit's planting – but not yet so fruitful.

And if anyone asks how they are to become stronger, I say it must be by the same process by which all things having life increase – they must grow. And this is what I mean by growth in grace.

I want men to look at growth in grace as a thing of infinite importance to the soul. In a more practical sense, our best interests would be met with a serious inquiry into the question of spiritual growth.

a) Growth in grace is the best evidence of spiritual health and prosperity. In a child or a flower or a tree, we are all aware that when there is no growth there is something wrong. Healthy life in an animal or vegetable will always show itself by progress and increase. It is just the same with our souls. If they are progressing and doing well, they will grow.

b) Growth in grace is one way to be happy in our religion. God has wisely linked together our comfort and our increase in holiness. He has graciously made it our interest to press on and aim high in our Christianity. There is a vast difference between the amount of sensible enjoyment which one believer has in his religion, compared to another. But you may be sure that ordinarily the man who feels the most joy and peace in believing and has the clearest witness of the Spirit in his heart is the man who grows.

c) Growth in grace is one secret of usefulness to others. Our influence on others for good depends greatly on what they see in us. The children of the world measure Christianity quite as much by their eyes as by their ears. The Christian who is always at a standstill, to all appearance the same man, with the same little faults and weaknesses and besetting sins and petty infirmities, is seldom the Christian who does much good. The man who shakes and stirs minds and sets the world thinking is the believer who is continually improving and going forward. Men think there is life and reality when they see growth.

d) Growth in grace pleases God. It may seem an astonishing thing, no doubt, that anything done by such creatures as we are can give pleasure to the Most High God. But so it is. The Scripture speaks of *walking* so as to please God. The Scripture says there are sacrifices with which 'God is pleased' (Heb. 13:16; see also 1 Thess. 4:1). The gardener loves to see the plants on which he has bestowed labour flourishing and bearing fruit. It cannot but disappoint and grieve him to see them stunted and standing still. Now what does our Lord Himself say? 'I am the true vine, and my Father is the gardener' (John 15:1); 'This is to my Father's glory, that you bear much fruit, showing yourselves to be my disciples' (John 15:8). The Lord takes pleasure in all His people – but especially in those who bear much fruit and grow.

e) Let us know, above all, that growth in grace is not only a thing *possible* – but a thing for which believers are *accountable*. To tell an unconverted man, dead in sins, to grow in grace would doubtless be absurd. To tell a believer, who is quickened and alive to God, to grow is only summoning him to a plain scriptural duty. He has a *new principle* within him, and it is a solemn duty not to quench it. Neglect of growth ...

robs him of privileges,

grieves the Spirit, and

makes the chariot wheels of his soul move heavily.

Whose fault is it, I would like to know, if a believer does not grow in grace? The fault, I am sure, cannot be laid on God. He delights to give more grace (Jas. 4:6); He 'delights in the well-being of his servant' (Ps. 35:27). The fault, no doubt, is our own. We ourselves are to blame, and none else, if we do not grow.

2. The marks of growth in grace

Let me take it for granted that we do not question the *reality* of growth in grace, and its vast *importance*. So far so good. But you now want to know *how* anyone may find out whether he is growing in grace or not? I answer that question, in the first place, by observing that we are very poor judges of our own condition, and that bystanders often know us better than we know ourselves. But I answer further that there are undoubtedly certain great marks and signs of growth in grace, and that wherever you see these marks you see a growing soul. I will now proceed to place some of these marks before you in order.

a) One mark of growth in grace is increased *humility*. The man whose soul is growing, feels his own sinfulness and unworthiness more every year.

He is ready to say with *Job*, 'I am unworthy',

And with *Abraham*, 'I am nothing but dust and ashes',

And with *Jacob*, 'I am unworthy of all the kindness',

And with *David*, 'I am a worm',

And with *Isaiah*, 'I am a man of unclean lips',

And with *Peter*, 'Lord ... I am a sinful man!'

(Job 40:4; Gen. 18:27; 32:10; Ps. 22:6; Isa. 6:5; Luke 5:8). The nearer he draws to God, and the more he sees of God's holiness and perfections, the more thoroughly is he sensible of his own countless sins and imperfections. The further he journeys in the way to heaven, the more he understands what Paul meant when he says,

'I am not already perfect!',

'I am the least of the apostles',

'I am less than the least of all the Lord's people',

'I am the worst [of sinners]'

(see Phil. 3:12; 1 Cor. 15:9; Eph. 3:8; 1 Tim. 1:15).

The riper he is for glory, the more, like the ripe corn, he hangs down his head. The brighter and clearer is his gospel light, the more he sees of the shortcomings and infirmities of his own heart. When first converted, he would tell you he saw but little of them, compared to what he sees now. Would anyone know whether he is growing in grace? Be sure that you look within for increased humility.

b) Another mark of growth in grace is increased *faith* and *love* towards our Lord Jesus Christ. The man whose soul is growing, finds more in Christ to rest upon every year, and rejoices more that he has such a Saviour. No doubt he saw much in Him when first he believed. His faith laid hold on the atonement of Christ, and gave him hope. But as he grows in grace, he sees a thousand things in Christ of which at first he never dreamed –

His love and power,

His heart and His intentions,

His offices as Substitute, Intercessor, Priest, Advocate, Physician, Shepherd and Friend

– unfold themselves to a growing soul in an unspeakable manner. In short, he discovers a suitableness in Christ to the needs of his soul, of which the half was once not known to him! Would anyone know if he is growing in grace? Then let him look within for increased knowledge of, and love to Christ.

c) Another mark of growth in grace is increased *holiness* of life and conduct. The man whose soul is growing, gets more dominion over sin, the world and the devil every year. He becomes more careful about ...

his temper,

his words, and

his actions. He is more watchful over his conduct in every relation of life. He strives more to be conformed to the image of Christ in all things, and to follow Him as his example, as well as to trust in Him as his Saviour. He is not content with old attainments and former grace. He forgets the things that are behind, and reaches forth unto those things which are before, making 'Higher!', 'Upward!', 'Forward!', 'Onward!' his continual motto (see Phil. 3:13). On earth, he thirsts and longs to have a will more entirely in unison with God's will. In heaven, the chief thing that he looks for, next to the presence of Christ, is complete separation from all sin. Would anyone know if he is growing in grace? Then let him look within for increased holiness.

d) Another mark of growth in grace is increased *spirituality* of taste and mind. The man whose soul is growing takes more interest in spiritual things every year. He does not neglect his duty in the world. He discharges faithfully, diligently and conscientiously every relation of life, whether at home or abroad. But the things he loves best are spiritual things. The amusements and recreations of the world have a continually decreasing place in his heart. He does not condemn them as downright sinful, nor say that those who have anything to do with them are going to hell. He only feels that they have a constantly diminishing hold on his own affections, and gradually seem smaller and more trifling in his eyes. Spiritual companions, spiritual occupations, spiritual conversation are of ever-increasing value to him. Would anyone know if he is growing in grace? Then let him look within for *increasing spirituality of taste*.

e) Another mark of growth in grace is increase in *love* to others. The man whose soul is growing is more full of love every year – of love to all men – but especially of love towards the brethren.

His love will show itself *actively* – in a growing disposition to do kindnesses, to take trouble for others, to be good-natured to everybody, to be generous, sympathizing, thoughtful, tender-hearted and considerate.

His love will show itself *passively* – in a growing disposition to be meek and patient towards all men, to put up with provocation and not stand upon his rights, to bear and forbear much rather than quarrel. A growing soul will try to put the best construction on other people's conduct, and to believe all things and hope all things, even to the end. There is no surer mark of backsliding and falling off in grace than an increasing disposition to find fault, pick holes and see weak points in others. Would anyone know if he is growing in grace? Then let him look within for increasing love to others.

f) One more mark of growth in grace is increased *zeal* and diligence in trying to do good to souls. The man who is really growing will take greater interest in the salvation of sinners every year. Missions at home and abroad, efforts of every kind to spread the gospel, attempts of any sort to increase gospel light and diminish gospel darkness – all these things will every year have a greater place in his attention.

He will not become 'weary in doing good' (Gal. 6:9; see 2 Thess. 3:13), just because he does not see every effort succeed. He will not care less for the progress of Christ's cause on earth as he grows older, though he will learn to expect less. He will just work on whatever the *result* may be – giving, praying, speaking, visiting, according to his position – and count his work its own reward. One of the surest marks of spiritual decline is a decreased interest about the souls of others, and the growth of Christ's kingdom. Would anyone know whether he is growing in grace? Then let him look within for *increased concern* about the salvation of souls.

Those high-flying religionists, whose only notion of Christianity is that of a state of perpetual joy and ecstasy, who tell you that they have got far beyond the region of conflict and soul-humiliation – such people no doubt will regard the marks I have laid down as 'legal', 'carnal' and 'tending to bondage'. I cannot help that. I call no man master in these things. I only wish my statements to be *tried in the balance of Scripture.*

And I firmly believe that what I have said is not only scriptural, but agreeable to the experience of the most eminent saints in every age. Show me a man in whom the six marks I have mentioned can be found. He is the man who can give a satisfactory answer to the question: 'Do we grow?' Such are the most trustworthy marks of growth in grace. Let us examine them carefully and consider what we ourselves know about them.

3. The means of growth in grace

The words of James must never be forgotten: 'Every good and perfect gift is from above, coming down from the Father of heavenly lights' (Jas. 1:17). This is no doubt as true of growth in grace as it is of everything else. It is the 'gift of God'. But still it must always be kept in mind that *God is pleased to work by means*. God has ordained means as well as ends. He who would grow in grace must use the means of growth.

This is a point, I fear, which is too much overlooked by believers. Many admire growth in grace in others, and wish that they themselves were like them. But they seem to suppose that those who grow are what they are by some special gift or grant from God – and that, as this gift is not bestowed on themselves, they must be content to sit still. This is a grievous delusion, and one against which I desire to testify with all my might. I wish it to be distinctly understood that growth in grace is bound up with the use of means within the reach of *all* believers, and that as a general rule, growing souls are what they are because they use these means.

Let me ask the special attention of my readers while I try to set forth in order the means of growth. Cast away forever the vain thought that if a believer does not grow in grace it is not his fault. Settle it in your mind that a believer, a man quickened by the Spirit, is not a mere dead creature but a being of mighty capacities and responsibilities. Let the words of Solomon sink down into your heart: '... the desires of the diligent are fully satisfied' (Prov. 13:4).

a) One thing essential to growth in grace is diligence in the use of *private* means of grace. By these I understand such means as a man must use by himself alone, and no one can use for him. I include under this head ...

private prayer,
private reading of the Scriptures,
private meditation, and
private self-examination.

The man who does not take pains about these things must never expect to grow. Here are the *roots* of true Christianity. Wrong here, and a man is wrong all the way through! Here is the whole reason why many professing Christians never seem to get on. They are careless and slovenly about their private *prayers*. They read their *Bibles*, but little and with very little heartiness of spirit. They give themselves no time for *self-inquiry* and *quiet thought* about the state of their souls.

It is useless to conceal from ourselves that the age we live in is full of peculiar dangers. It is an age of great activity – and of much hurry, bustle and excitement in religion. Many are running 'here and there', no doubt, 'to increase knowledge' (Dan. 12:4). Thousands are ready enough for public meetings, sermon hearing, or anything else in which there is 'sensation'. Few appear to remember the absolute necessity of making time to 'search your hearts and be silent' (Ps. 4:4). But without this, there is seldom any deep spiritual prosperity. Let us remember this point! Private religion must receive our first attention, if we wish our souls to grow.

b) Another thing which is essential to growth in grace is carefulness in the use of *public* means of grace. By these I understand such means as a man has within his reach as a member of Christ's visible church. Under this head I include the ordinances of regular Sunday worship, the uniting with God's people in common prayer and praise, the preaching of the Word and the sacrament of the Lord's Supper.

I firmly believe that the manner in which these public means of grace are used has much to say to the prosperity of a believer's soul. It is easy to use them in a cold and heartless way. The very familiarity of them is apt to make us careless. The regular return of the same voice, and the same kind of words, and the same ceremonies is likely to make us sleepy and callous and unfeeling. Here is a snare into which too many professing Christians fall. If we would grow, we must be on our guard here. Here is a matter in which the Spirit is often grieved, and saints receive great damage. Let us strive to use the old prayers, and sing the old hymns, and kneel at the old communion rail, and hear the old truths preached – with as much freshness and appetite as in the year we first believed.

It is a sign of bad health when a person loses relish for his food; and it is a sign of spiritual decline when we lose our appetite for means of grace. Whatever we do about public means, let us always 'do it with all [our] might' (Eccl. 9:10). This is the way to grow!

c) Another thing essential to growth in grace is *watchfulness over our conduct* in the little matters of everyday life. Our tempers, our tongues, the discharge of our several relations of life, our employment of time – each and all must be vigilantly attended to, if we wish our souls to prosper. Life is made up of days, and days of hours, and the little things of every hour are never so little as to be beneath the care of a Christian. When a tree begins to decay at root or heart, the mischief is first seen at the extreme end of the little branches. 'He who despises little things,' says an uninspired writer, 'shall fall little by little.' That witness is true. Let others despise us, if they like, and call us precise and overly careful. Let us patiently hold on our way, remembering that *we serve a precise God*, that our Lord's example is to be copied in the least things as well as the greatest; and that we must take up our cross daily and hourly, rather than sin. We must aim to have a Christianity which, like the sap of a tree, runs through every twig and leaf of our character, and sanctifies all. This is one way to grow!

d) Another thing which is essential to growth in grace is caution about the *company* we keep and the *friendships* we form. Nothing perhaps affects man's character more than the company he keeps. We catch the ways and tone of those we live and talk with, and unhappily get harm far more easily than good. Disease is infectious – but health is not!

Now, if a professing Christian deliberately chooses to be intimate with those who are not friends of God, and who cling to the world, his soul is sure to be harmed. It is hard enough to serve Christ under any circumstances, in such an evil world as this. But it is doubly hard to do it if we are close friends of the thoughtless and ungodly. Mistakes in friendship or marriage engagements are the whole reason why some have entirely ceased to grow. 'Do not be misled: "Bad company corrupts good character"' (1 Cor. 15:33); '... friendship with the world means enmity against God' (Jas. 4:4). Let us seek friends who will stir us up about ...

our prayers, our Bible-reading, and our employment of time;

our souls, our salvation, and the world to come.

Who can tell the good that a friend's word in season may do, or the harm that it may stop? This is one way to grow.

e) There is one more thing which is absolutely essential to growth in grace, and that is regular and habitual *communion with the Lord Jesus*. In saying this, let no one suppose for a minute that I am referring to the Lord's Supper. I mean nothing of the kind. I mean that daily habit of communion between the believer and his Saviour, which can only be carried on by faith, prayer and meditation. It is a habit, I fear, of which many believers know little. A man may be a believer and have his feet on the Rock and yet live far below his privileges. It is possible to have 'union' with Christ and yet to have little if any 'communion' with Him. But, for all that, there is such a thing.

The names and offices of Christ, as laid down in Scripture, appear to me to show unmistakably that this communion between the saint and his Saviour is not mere imagination, but a real true thing.

Between the Bridegroom – and His bride,

between the Head – and His members,

between the Physician – and His patients,

between the Advocate – and His clients,

between the Shepherd – and His sheep,

between the Master – and His scholars –

there is evidently implied a habit ...

of familiar communion,

of daily application for things needed,

of daily pouring out and unburdening our hearts and minds.

Such a habit of dealing with Christ is clearly something more than a vague general trust in the work that Christ did for sinners. It is getting close to Him and laying hold on Him with confidence as *a loving, personal Friend*. This is what I mean by communion.

Now I believe that no man will ever grow in grace, who does not know something experimentally of the habit of communion. We must not be content with a general orthodox knowledge that Christ is the

Mediator between God and man, and that justification is by faith and not by works, and that we put our trust in Christ. We must go further than this. We must seek to have *personal intimacy* with the Lord Jesus, and to deal with Him as a man deals with a loving friend. We must realize what it is ...

to turn to Him first in every need,

to talk to Him about every difficulty,

to consult Him about every step,

to spread before Him all our sorrows,

to get Him to share in all our joys,

to do all as in His sight, and

to go through every day leaning on and looking to Him.

This is the way that Paul lived: 'The life I now live in the body, I live by faith in the Son of God' (Gal. 2:20); '... to me, to live is Christ' (Phil. 1:21). It is ignorance of this way of living which makes so many see no beauty in the book of Canticles. But it is the man who lives in this way who keeps up constant communion with Christ – this is the man, I say emphatically, whose soul will grow!

Practical applications

Although much more could be said on this weighty subject, let us now turn to some *practical applications* keeping in mind its tremendous importance.

1. This text may fall into the hands of some who know *nothing* whatever about growth in grace. They have little or no concern about religion. A little Sunday church-going or chapel-going makes up the sum and substance of their Christianity. They are without spiritual life – so of course they cannot at present grow. Are you one of these people? If you are, you are in a pitiable condition.

Years are slipping away, and time is flying. Graveyards are filling up, and families are thinning. Death and judgement are getting nearer to us all. And yet you live like one *asleep* about your soul. What madness! What folly! What *suicide* can be worse than this?

Awake before it is too late; awake, and arise from the dead, and live to God. Turn to Him who is sitting at the right hand of God, to be your Saviour and Friend. Turn to Christ, and cry mightily to Him about your soul. There is yet hope! He who called Lazarus from the grave has not changed. He who commanded the widow's son at Nain to arise from his casket can do miracles yet for your soul. Seek Him at once: seek Christ, if you would not be lost forever. Do not stand still *talking* and *meaning* and *intending* and *wishing* and *hoping*. Seek Christ that you may *live*; and that living, you may *grow*.

2. This text may fall into the hands of some who *should* know something of growth in grace – but at present know nothing at all. They have made little or no progress since they were first converted. They seem 'complacent' (Zeph. 1:12). They go on from year to year content with old grace, old experience, old knowledge, old faith, old measure of attainment, old religious expressions, old set phrases. Like the Gibeonites, their bread is always mouldy, and their shoes are patched and clouted. They never appear to progress. Are you one of these people? If you are, you are living far below your privileges and responsibilities. It is high time to examine yourself!

If you have reason to hope that you are a true believer, and yet do not grow in grace, there must be a fault, and a serious fault somewhere! It cannot be the will of God that your soul should stand still. '... he gives us more grace'; He 'delights in the well-being of his servant' (Jas. 4:6; Ps. 35:27). It cannot be for your own happiness or usefulness that your soul should stand still. Without growth, you will never rejoice in the Lord (Phil. 4:4). Without growth, you will never do good to others. Surely this lack of growth is a serious matter! It should raise in you great searchings of heart. There must be 'words spoken gently' (Job 15:11). There must be some cause!

Take the advice I give you. Resolve this very day that you will find out the reason of your standstill condition. Probe every corner of your soul, with a faithful and firm hand. Search from one end of the camp to the other, until you find out the Achan who is weakening you! Begin with an application to the Lord Jesus Christ, the great Physician of souls, and ask Him to heal the secret ailment within you, whatever it may be. Begin as if you had never applied to Him before, and ask for grace to cut off the right hand and pluck out the right eye. But never, never be content – if your soul does not grow.

For your peace's sake,

for your usefulness's sake,

for the honour of your Maker's cause –

resolve to find out the reason why!

3. This message may fall into the hands of some who are *really* growing in grace but are not aware of it, and will not allow it. Their very growth is the reason why they do not see their growth! Their continual increase in humility prevents them feeling that they advance. Like Moses, when he came down from the mount from communing with God, their faces shine. And yet, like Moses, they are not aware of it (Exod. 34:29). Such Christians, I grant freely, are not common. But here and there such are to be found. Like angels' visits, they are few and far between. Happy is the neighbourhood where such growing Christians live! To meet them and see them and be in their company is like meeting and seeing a bit of 'heaven upon earth'.

Now what shall I say to such people? What can I say? What ought I to say? Shall I bid them awake to a consciousness of their own growth, and be pleased with it? I will do nothing of the kind! Shall I tell them to plume themselves on their own attainments, and look at their own superiority to others? God forbid! I will do nothing of the kind. To tell them such things would do them no good. To tell them such things, above all, would be a useless waste of time.

If there is any one feature about a growing soul which specially marks him, it is his *deep sense of his own unworthiness*. He never sees anything to be praised in himself. He only feels that he is an unprofitable servant and the chief of sinners. It is the godly, in the picture of the judgement day, who say, 'Lord, when did we see you hungry and feed you ...?' (Matt. 25:37). Extremes do indeed meet strangely sometimes. The conscience-hardened sinner and the eminent saint are in one respect singularly alike. Neither of them fully realizes his own condition. The one does not see his own sin, nor the other his own grace!

But shall I say nothing to *growing* Christians? Is there no word of counsel I can address to them? The sum and substance of all that I can say is to be found in two sentences: 'Go forward!'; 'Press on!'

We can never have ...

too much *humility*,

too much *faith* in Christ,

149

too much *holiness*,

too much *spirituality* of mind,

too much *love*,

too much *zeal* in doing good to others.

Then let us be continually forgetting the things behind, and reaching forth unto the things before (Phil. 3:13). The best of Christians in these matters is infinitely below the perfect pattern of his Lord. Whatever the world may please to say, we may be sure there is no danger of any of us becoming *too holy*.

Let us cast to the winds as idle talk the common notion that it is possible to be 'extreme' and go 'too far' in religion. This is a favourite lie of the devil and one which he circulates with vast industry. No doubt there are enthusiasts and fanatics to be found, who bring an evil report upon Christianity by their extravagances and follies. But if anyone means to say that a mortal man can be too humble, too charitable, too holy or too diligent in doing good, he must either be an infidel or a fool. In serving pleasure and money, it is easy to go too far. But in following the things which make up true religion and in serving Christ, there can be no extreme.

Let us never measure our religion by that of others, and think we are doing enough, if we have gone beyond our neighbours. This is another snare of the devil. Let us mind our own business. '... what is that to you?' said our Master on a certain occasion. 'You must follow me' (John 21:22). Let us follow on, aiming at nothing short of perfection. Let us follow on, making Christ's life and character our only pattern and example. Let us follow on, remembering daily that *at our best* we are but miserable sinners. Let us follow on, and never forget that it signifies nothing whether we are better than others or not. At our very best we are far worse than we ought to be. There will always be room for improvement in us. We shall be *debtors to Christ's mercy and grace* to the very last. Then let us leave off looking at others, and comparing ourselves with others. We shall find enough to do, if we look at our own hearts.

Last, but not least, if we know anything of growth in grace and desire to know more, let us not be surprised if we have to go through much trial and affliction in this world. I firmly believe it is the experience of nearly all the most eminent saints. Like their blessed Master, they have been men of sorrows, acquainted with grief and perfected through sufferings (Isa. 53:3; Heb. 2:10). It is a striking saying of our Lord, '... every branch in me ... that does bear fruit he prunes so that it will be even more fruitful' (John 15:2). It is a melancholy fact that *constant temporal prosperity*, as a general rule, is *injurious* to a believer's soul. We cannot grow under it. Sicknesses and losses and crosses and anxieties and disappointments seem absolutely needful to keep us humble, watchful and spiritual-minded. They are as needful as the pruning knife to the vine, and the refiner's furnace to the gold. They are not pleasant to flesh and blood. We do not like them, and often do not see their meaning. 'No discipline seems pleasant *at the time*, but painful. Later on, however, it produces a harvest of righteousness' (Heb. 12:11, italics mine). We shall find that all worked for our good when we reach heaven.

Let these thoughts abide in our minds, if we love growth in grace. When days of darkness come upon us, let us not count it a strange thing. Rather let us remember that lessons are learned on such days, which would never have been learned in sunshine. Let us say to ourselves, 'This also is for my profit, that I may be a partaker of God's holiness. It is sent in love. I am in *God's best school*. Correction is instruction. This is meant to make me grow!'

I leave the subject of growth in grace here. I trust I have said enough to set some readers thinking about it.

All things are growing older – the world is growing old; we ourselves are growing older. A few more summers, a few more winters, a few more sicknesses, a few more sorrows, a few more weddings, a few more funerals, a few more meetings and a few more partings, and then – what? *Why, the grass will be growing over our graves!*

7

Assurance

'For I am already being poured out like
a drink offering, and the time for my
departure is near. I have fought the good
fight, I have finished the race, I have kept
the faith. Now there is in store for me the
crown of righteousness, which the Lord, the
righteous Judge, will award to me on that
day – and not only to me, but also to all
who have longed for his appearing.'

(2 Tim. 4:6–8)

Here we see the apostle Paul looking three ways: downward, backward, forward –

downward to the grave,

backward to his own ministry,

forward to that great day, the day of judgement!

It will do us good to stand by the apostle's side a few minutes and mark the words he uses. Happy is that soul who can look where Paul looked and then speak as Paul spoke!

1. He looks *downward* to the grave – and he does it without fear.

Hear what he says: 'I am ... ready to be offered' (2 Tim. 4:6, KJV). I am like an animal brought to the place of sacrifice and bound with cords to the very horns of the altar. The drink offering, which generally accompanies the oblation, is already being poured out. The last ceremonies have been gone through. Every preparation has been made. It only remains to receive the death-blow – and then all is over.

'... the time for my departure is near.' I am like a ship about to unmoor and put to sea. All on board is ready. I only wait to have the moorings cast off that fasten me to the shore – and I shall then set sail and begin my voyage.

These are remarkable words to come from the lips of a child of Adam like ourselves! Death is a solemn thing, and never so much so as when we see it close at hand. The grave is a chilling, heart-sickening place, and it is vain to pretend it has no terrors. Yet here is a mortal man who can look calmly into the narrow house appointed for all living, and say, while he stands upon the brink, 'I see it all – and am not afraid!' Let us listen to him again:

2. He looks *backward* to his ministerial life – and he does it without shame.

Hear what he says: 'I have fought the good fight ...' There he speaks as a soldier. I have fought that good fight with the world, the flesh and the devil – from which so many shrink and draw back.

'... I have finished the race ...' There he speaks as a runner for a prize. I have run the race marked out for me. I have gone over the ground appointed for me, however rough and steep. I have not turned aside because of difficulties, nor been discouraged by the length of the way. I am at last in sight of the goal.

'... I have kept the faith ...' There he speaks as a steward. I have held fast that glorious gospel which was committed to my trust. I have not mingled it with man's traditions, nor spoiled its simplicity by adding my own inventions, nor allowed others to adulterate it without withstanding them to the face. 'As a soldier, a runner, a steward,' he seems to say, 'I am not ashamed.'

That Christian is happy who, as he leaves the world, can leave such testimony behind him. A good conscience will ...

save no man,

wash away no sin,

not lift us one hair's breadth towards heaven.

Yet a good conscience will be found a pleasant visitor at our bedside in a dying hour. There is a fine passage in *The Pilgrim's Progress* which describes old Honest's passage across the river of death. 'Now the River,' says Bunyan, 'at that time overflowed the banks in some places. But Mr Honest in his life-time had spoken to one Good-conscience to meet him there, the which he also did, and lent him his hand, and so helped him over.' We may be sure, there is a mine of truth in that passage. Let us hear the apostle once more:

3. He looks *forward* to the great day of reckoning – and he does it without doubt.

Mark his words: 'Now there is in store for me the crown of righteousness, which the Lord, the righteous Judge, will award to me on that day – and not only to me, but also to all who have longed for his appearing.' 'A glorious reward,' he seems to say, 'is ready and laid up in store for me – even that crown which is only given to the righteous. In the great day of judgement the Lord shall give this crown to me, and to all who have loved Him as an unseen Saviour, and longed to see Him face to face. My work on earth is over. This one thing now remains for me to look forward to, and nothing more.'

Let us observe that the apostle speaks without any hesitation or distrust. He regards the crown as a sure thing – as his own already. He declares with unfaltering confidence his firm persuasion that the righteous Judge will give it to him. Paul was no stranger to all the circumstances and accompaniments of that solemn day to which he referred. The great white throne, the assembled world, the open books, the revealing of all secrets, the listening angels, the solemn sentence, the eternal separation of the lost and saved – all these were things with which he was well acquainted. But none of these things moved him. His strong faith overleaped them all and saw only Jesus, his all-prevailing Advocate, and the blood of sprinkling and sin washed away. 'A crown,' he says, 'is laid up for me; the Lord Himself shall give it to me.' He speaks as if he saw it all with his own eyes!

Such are the main things which these verses contain. Of most of them I shall not speak, because I want to confine myself to the special subject of this exposition. I shall only try to consider one point in the passage. That point is the strong 'assurance of hope' with which the apostle looks forward to his own prospects in the day of judgement.

I shall consider it readily, and at the same time with fear and trembling. I feel that I am treading on very difficult ground and that it is easy to speak rashly and unscripturally in this matter. The road between truth and error is here especially a narrow pass, and if I shall be enabled to do good to some without doing harm to others, I shall be very thankful.

I shall lay out the scriptural reality for an assured hope, as well as explain that some are saved who never attain it. Also, I will explain why assurance is desirable – and remark on why it is so seldom acquired.

If I am not greatly mistaken, there is a very close connection between true holiness and assurance. Before I close this message, I hope to show my readers the nature of that connection. At present, I content myself with saying that where there is the most *holiness* there is generally the most *assurance*.

An assured hope is a true and scriptural thing

Assurance, such as Paul expresses in the verses which head this message, is not a mere feeling or figment of the imagination. It is not the result of high animal spirits, or an expectant temperament of mind. It is a positive gift of the Holy Spirit, bestowed without reference to men's bodily frames or constitutions, and a gift which every believer in Christ ought to aim at and seek after.

In matters like these, the first question is this: 'What says the Scripture?' I answer that question without the least hesitation. The

Word of God appears to me to teach distinctly that *a believer may arrive at an assured confidence with regard to his own salvation.*

I lay it down fully and broadly, as God's truth, that a true Christian, a converted man may reach such a comfortable degree of faith in Christ that in general he shall feel entirely confident as to the pardon and safety of his soul, shall seldom be troubled with doubts, seldom be distracted with fears, seldom be distressed by anxious questionings and, in short, though vexed by many an inward conflict with sin, shall look forward to death without trembling, and to judgement without dismay. This, I say, is the doctrine of the Bible.

Such is my account of assurance. I will ask my readers to mark it well. I say neither less nor more than I have here laid down. Now such a statement as this is often disputed and denied. Many cannot see the truth of it at all.

The church of Rome denounces assurance in the most unmeasured terms. The Council of Trent declares roundly that a 'believer's assurance of the pardon of his sins, is a vain and ungodly confidence', and Cardinal Bellarmine, the well-known champion of Romanism, calls it 'a prime error of heretics'.

The vast majority of the worldly and thoughtless Christians among ourselves oppose the doctrine of assurance. It offends and annoys them to hear of it. They do not like others to feel comfortable and sure, because they never feel so themselves. Ask them whether their sins are forgiven, and they will probably tell you they do not know! That they cannot receive the doctrine of assurance is certainly no marvel.

But there are also some true believers who reject assurance or shrink from it as a doctrine fraught with danger. They consider it borders on presumption. They seem to think it a proper humility never to feel sure, never to be confident and to live in a certain degree of doubt and suspense about their souls. This is to be regretted and does much harm.

I frankly allow there are some presumptuous people who profess to feel a confidence for which they have no scriptural warrant. There are always some people who think well of themselves when God thinks ill, just as there are some who think ill of themselves when God thinks well. There always will be such. *There never yet was a scriptural truth without abuses and counterfeits.* God's election, man's impotence, salvation by grace – all are alike abused. There will be fanatics and enthusiasts as long as the world stands. But, for all this, assurance is a reality and a true thing; and God's children must not let themselves be driven from the use of a truth – merely because it is abused.

My answer to all who deny the existence of real, well-grounded assurance is simply this: 'What says the Scripture?' If assurance is not there, I have not another word to say.

But does not Job say, 'I *know* that my redeemer lives, and that in the end he will stand on the earth. And after my skin has been destroyed, yet in my flesh I will see God' (Job 19:25,26, italics mine).

Does not David say, 'Even though I walk through the darkest valley, I will fear no evil, for you are with me; your rod and your staff, they comfort me' (Ps. 23:4).

Does not Isaiah say, 'You will keep in perfect peace those whose minds are steadfast, because they trust in you' (Isa. 26:3).

And again, 'The fruit of that righteousness will be peace; its effect will be quietness and confidence for ever' (Isa. 32:17).

Does not Paul say to the Romans, 'I am convinced that neither death nor life, neither angels nor demons, neither the present nor the future, nor any powers, neither height nor depth, nor anything else in all creation, will be able to separate us from the love of God that is in Christ Jesus our Lord' (Rom. 8:38,39).

Does he not say to the Corinthians, '... we know that if the earthly tent we live in is destroyed, we have a building from God, an eternal house in heaven, not built by human hands' (2 Cor. 5:1).

And again, '... we are always confident and know that as long as we are at home in the body we are away from the Lord' (2 Cor. 5:6).

Does he not say to Timothy, 'I know whom I have believed, and am convinced that he is able to guard what I have entrusted to him' (2 Tim. 1:12).

And does he not speak to the Colossians of 'the full assurance of understanding' (Col. 2:2, KJV), and to the Hebrews of 'the full assurance that faith brings' and 'the full assurance of hope' (Heb. 10:22; 6:11, KJV).

Does not Peter say expressly, '... make every effort to confirm your calling and election' (2 Pet. 1:10).

Does not John say, 'We know that we have passed from death to life' (1 John 3:14).

And again, 'I write these things to you who believe in the name of the Son of God so that you may *know* that you have eternal life' (1 John 5:13, italics mine).

And again, 'We *know* that we are children of God' (1 John 5:19, italics mine).

What shall we say to these things? I desire to speak with all humility on any controverted point. I feel that I am only a poor fallible child of Adam myself. But I must say that in the passages I have just quoted, I see something far higher than the mere 'hopes' and 'trusts' with which so many believers appear content in this day. I see the language of persuasion, confidence, knowledge – no, I may almost say, of certainty. And I feel, for my own part, if I may take these Scriptures in their plain obvious meaning, the doctrine of assurance is true.

But my answer, also, to all who dislike the doctrine of assurance as bordering on presumption, is this: it can hardly be presumption to tread in the steps of Peter and Paul, of Job and of John. They were all eminently humble and lowly minded men, if ever any were, and yet they all speak of their own state with an assured hope. Surely this should teach us that *deep humility* and *strong assurance* are perfectly compatible, and that there is not any necessary connection between spiritual confidence and pride.

My answer, furthermore, is that many have attained to such an assured hope as our text expresses, even in modern times. I will not concede for a moment that it was a peculiar privilege confined to the apostolic day. There have been in our own land many believers who have appeared to walk in almost uninterrupted fellowship with the Father and the Son, who have seemed to enjoy an almost unceasing sense of the light of God's reconciled countenance shining down upon them, and have left their experience on record. I could mention well-known names, if space permitted. The thing has been, and is – and that is enough.

My answer, lastly, is: it cannot be wrong to feel confidently in a matter where God speaks unconditionally; to believe decidedly when God promises decidedly; to have a sure persuasion of pardon and peace when we rest on the word and oath of Him who never changes. It is an utter mistake to suppose that the believer who feels assurance is resting on anything he sees in himself. He simply leans on the Mediator of the New Covenant and the Scripture of truth. He believes the Lord Jesus means what He says and takes Him at His word. *Assurance*, after all, is no more than a *full-grown faith* – a masculine faith that grasps Christ's promise with both hands; a faith that argues like the good centurion, 'If the Lord speaks the word only, I am healed. Why then should I doubt?' (see Matt. 8:8).

We may be sure that Paul was the last man in the world to build his assurance on any works of his own. He who could write himself down as 'chief of sinners' (see 1 Tim. 1:15), and had a deep sense of his own guilt and corruption. But then he had a still deeper sense of the length and breadth of Christ's righteousness imputed to him. He who could cry, 'What a wretched man I am!' (Rom. 7:24), had a clear view of the fountain of evil within his heart. But then he had a still clearer view of that other Fountain which can remove all sin and uncleanness. He who thought himself 'less than the least of all the Lord's people' (Eph. 3:8) had a lively and abiding feeling of his own weakness. But he had a still livelier feeling that Christ's promise, 'My sheep ... shall never perish' (John 10:27,28), could not be broken.

Paul knew, if ever man did, that he was a poor, frail bark, floating on a stormy ocean. He saw, if any did, the rolling waves and roaring tempest by which he was surrounded. But then he looked away from *self* to *Jesus* – and was not afraid. He remembered that anchor within the veil, which is both 'firm and secure' (Heb. 6:19). He remembered the word and work and constant intercession of Him who loved him and gave Himself for him. And this it was, and nothing else, which enabled him to say so boldly, 'A crown is laid up for me, and the Lord shall give it to me,' and to conclude so surely, 'The Lord will preserve me: I shall never be confounded.'

A believer may *never* arrive at this assured hope – and yet be saved

I would not desire to make one contrite heart sad that God has not made sad, or to discourage one fainting child of God, or to leave the impression that men have no part or lot in Christ – unless they feel assurance.

A person may have saving faith in Christ and yet never enjoy an assured hope, such as the apostle Paul enjoyed. To believe and have a glimmering hope of acceptance is one thing; to have 'joy and peace' in our believing, and abound in hope, is quite another. *All God's children have faith – but not all have assurance.* I think this ought never to be forgotten.

I know some great and good men have held a different opinion. I believe that many excellent ministers of the gospel, at whose feet I would gladly sit, do not allow the distinction I have stated. But I desire to call no man master. I dread as much as anyone the idea of healing the wounds of conscience slightly, but I would think any other view than what I have given to be a most uncomfortable gospel to preach, and one very likely to keep souls back a long time from the gate of life.

I do not shrink from saying that by grace a man may have sufficient faith to flee to Christ – sufficient faith really to lay hold on Him, really to trust in Him, really to be a child of God, really to be

163

saved – and yet to his last day be never free from much anxiety, doubt and fear.

'A letter,' says an old writer, 'may be written, which is not sealed; so grace may be written in the heart – yet the Spirit may not set the seal of assurance to it.'

A child may be born heir to a great fortune, and yet never be aware of his riches, may live childish, die childish and never know the greatness of his possessions. And so also a man may be a babe in Christ's family, think as a babe, speak as a babe and, though saved, never enjoy a lively hope or know the real privileges of his inheritance.

Let no man mistake my meaning, when I dwell strongly on the *reality, privilege* and *importance* of assurance. Do not do me the injustice to say, I teach that none are saved unless such as can say with Paul, 'I know ... and am convinced' that 'there is in store for me the crown of righteousness' (2 Tim. 1:12; 2 Tim. 4:8). I do not say so. I teach nothing of the kind.

Faith in the Lord Jesus Christ a man must have, beyond all question, if he is to be saved. I know no other way of access to the Father. I see no intimation of mercy, excepting through Christ. A man must feel his sins and lost estate, must come to Jesus for pardon and salvation, must rest his hope on Him, and on Him alone. But if he only has faith to do this, however weak and feeble that faith may be, I will engage, as Scripture warrants, he shall not miss heaven.

Never, never let us curtail the freeness of the glorious gospel, or clip its fair proportions. Never let us make the gate smaller and the way more narrow than pride and the love of sin have made it already. The Lord Jesus is very pitiful and of tender mercy. He does not regard the quantity of faith, but the quality. He does not measure its degree, but its reality. He will not break any bruised reed, nor quench any smoking flax. He will never let it be said that any perished at the foot of the cross. '... whoever comes to me,' He says, 'I will never drive away' (John 6:37).

Yes! Though a man's faith is no bigger than a grain of mustard seed, if it only brings him to Christ, and enables him to touch the hem of His garment, he shall be saved – saved as surely as the oldest saint in paradise, saved as completely and eternally as Peter or John or Paul. There are degrees in our sanctification. In our justification there are none. What is written is written and shall never fail: 'Anyone who *believes* in him' – not whoever has a *strong* and *mighty* faith – 'Anyone who *believes* in him will never be put to shame' (Rom. 10:11, italics mine).

But all this time, be it remembered, the poor believing soul may have no full assurance of his pardon and acceptance with God. He may be troubled with fear upon fear and doubt upon doubt. He may have many an inward question and many an anxiety, many a struggle and many a misgiving, clouds and darkness, storm and tempest to the very end.

Bare simple faith in Christ shall save a man, though he may never attain to assurance; but will it bring him to heaven with strong and abounding consolations? I will concede that it shall land him safe in harbour; but I will not concede that he will enter that harbour in full sail, confident and rejoicing. I would not be surprised if he reaches his desired haven weather-beaten and tempest-tossed, scarcely realizing his own safety – until he opens his eyes in glory.

We should carefully note these simple distinctions between faith and assurance. It is all too easy to confuse the two. Faith, let us remember, is the root, and assurance is the flower. Doubtless you can never have the flower without the root; but it is no less certain you may have the root and not the flower.

Faith is that poor trembling woman who came behind Jesus as the crowd were pressing round him, and touched the hem of His garment (Mark 5:25). Assurance is Stephen standing calmly in the midst of his murderers and saying, 'I see heaven open and the Son of Man standing at the right hand of God' (Acts 7:56).

Faith is the penitent thief, crying, 'Jesus, remember me' (Luke 23:42). Assurance is Job, sitting in the dust, covered with sores, and saying, 'I know that my redeemer lives' (Job 19:25); 'Though he slay me, yet will I hope in him' (Job 13:15).

Faith is Peter's drowning cry, as he began to sink: 'Lord, save me!' (Matt. 14:30). Assurance is that same Peter declaring before the council in after times, 'Salvation is found in no one else, for there is no other name under heaven given to mankind by which we must be saved' (Acts 4:12).

Faith is the anxious, trembling voice: 'I do believe; help me overcome my unbelief!' (Mark 9:24). Assurance is the confident challenge: 'Who will bring any charge against those whom God has chosen? ... Who then is the one who condemns?' (Rom. 8:33,34).

Faith is Saul praying in the house of Judas at Damascus, sorrowful, blind and alone (Acts 9:11). Assurance is Paul, the aged prisoner, looking calmly into the grave, and saying, 'I know whom I have believed' and 'there is in store for me the crown of righteousness' (2 Tim. 1:12; 4:8).

Faith is life. How great the blessing! Who can describe or realize the great *gulf* between life and death? '... even a live dog is better off than a dead lion!' (Eccl. 9:4). And yet life may be weak, sickly, unhealthy, painful, trying, anxious, weary, burdensome, joyless and smileless to the very end. *Assurance is more than life*. It is health, strength, power, vigour, activity, energy, manliness, beauty.

It is not a question of 'saved – or not saved' that lies before us, but of 'privilege – or no privilege'. It is not a question of peace – or no peace, but of great peace – or little peace. It is not a question between the wanderers of this world and the school of Christ; it is one that belongs only to the school: it is between the first grade and the highest grade.

He who has *faith* does well. Happy would I be, if I thought all readers of this message had it. Blessed, thrice blessed, are those who believe! They are safe. They are washed. They are justified. They are beyond the power of hell. Satan, with all his malice, shall never pluck them out of Christ's hand. But he who has *assurance* does far better – sees more, feels more, knows more, enjoys more, has more days like those spoken of in Deuteronomy, even 'the days that the heavens are above the earth' (Deut. 11:21).

Reasons why an assured hope is exceedingly to be desired

I ask special attention to this point. I heartily wish that assurance was more sought after than it is. Too many among those who believe begin doubting and go on doubting, live doubting and die doubting, and *go to heaven in a kind of mist*.

It would ill befit me to speak in a slighting way of 'hopes'. But I fear many of us sit down content with them and go no further. I would like to see fewer 'perhaps' in the Lord's family and more who could say, 'I know and am persuaded.' Oh, that all believers would covet the *best* gifts, and not be content with less! Many miss the full tide of blessedness the gospel was meant to convey. Many keep themselves in a low and starved condition of soul, while their Lord is saying, 'Eat, friends, and drink; drink your fill of love'; 'Ask and you will receive, and your joy will be complete' (Song 5:1; John 16:24).

1. Let us remember that assurance is to be desired, because of the present comfort and peace it affords. Doubts and fears have power to spoil much of the happiness of a true believer in Christ. Uncertainty and suspense are bad enough in any condition – in the matter of our health, our property, our families, our affections, our earthly callings – but never so bad as in the affairs of our souls. And so long as a believer cannot get beyond 'I hope', he manifestly feels a degree of uncertainty about his spiritual state. The very words imply as much. He says 'I hope' because he dares not say 'I know'.

Now, assurance goes far to set a child of God free from this painful kind of bondage, and thus ministers mightily to his comfort. It enables him to feel that the great business of life – is a settled business, the great debt – a paid debt, the great disease – a healed disease, and the great work – a finished work; and all other business, diseases, debts and works are then by comparison small. In this way, assurance makes him ...

patient in tribulation,
calm under bereavements,
unmoved in sorrow,
not afraid of evil tidings,

in every condition content –

for it gives him a fixedness of heart.

Assurance ...

sweetens his bitter cups,

lessens the burden of his crosses,

smoothes the rough places over which he travels,

enlightens the valley of the shadow of death.

It makes him always feel that he has something solid beneath his feet and something firm under his hands – a *sure friend* by the way, and a *sure home* at the end.

Assurance will help a man to bear poverty and loss. It will teach him to say, 'I know that I have in heaven a better and more enduring substance. Silver and gold have I none, but grace and glory are mine, and these can never make themselves wings and flee away. Though the fig tree shall not blossom – yet I will rejoice in the Lord' (see Hab. 3:17,18).

Assurance will support a child of God under the heaviest bereavements and assist him to feel 'It is well'. An assured soul will say, 'Though beloved ones are taken from me, yet Jesus is the same, and is alive for evermore. Christ, being raised from the dead, dies no more. Though my house is not as flesh and blood could wish – yet I have "an everlasting covenant, arranged and secure in every part"' (see 2 Kgs. 4:26; see Heb. 13:8; see Rom. 6:9; 2 Sam. 23:5).

Assurance will enable a man to praise God and be thankful, even in prison, like Paul and Silas at Philippi. It can give a believer songs even in the darkest night and joy when all things seem going against him (Job 35:10; Ps. 42:8).

Assurance will enable a man to sleep with the full prospect of death on the morrow, like Peter in Herod's dungeon. It will teach him to say, 'In peace I will lie down and sleep, for you alone, LORD, make me dwell in safety' (Ps. 4:8).

Assurance can make a man rejoice to suffer shame for Christ's sake, as the apostles did when put in prison at Jerusalem (Acts 5:41). It will remind him that he may 'Rejoice and be glad' (Matt. 5:12), and there is in heaven, an exceeding weight of glory that shall make amends for all (2 Cor. 4:17).

Assurance will enable a believer to meet a violent and painful death without fear, as Stephen did in the beginning of Christ's church, and as Cranmer, Ridley, Hooper, Latimer, Rogers and Taylor did in our own land. It will bring to his heart the texts: '... do not be afraid of those who kill the body and after that can do no more' (Luke 12:4); 'Lord Jesus, receive my spirit' (Acts 7:59).

Assurance will support a man in pain and sickness, make all his bed, and smooth down his dying pillow. It will enable him to say, '... if the earthly tent we live in is destroyed, we have a building from God' (2 Cor. 5:1); 'I desire to depart and be with Christ' (Phil. 1:23); 'My flesh and my heart may fail, but God is the strength of my heart and my portion for ever' (Ps. 73:26).

The strong consolation which assurance can give in the hour of death is a point of great importance. We may depend on it, we shall never think assurance so precious as when our turn comes to die. In that solemn hour there are few believers who do not find out the value and privilege of an 'assured hope', whatever they may have thought about it during their lives. General 'hopes' and 'trusts' are all very well to live upon while the sun shines and the body is strong; but when we come to die, we shall want to be able to say, 'I know' and 'I feel'. The river of death is a cold stream – and we have to cross it alone. No earthly friend can help us. The last enemy, the king of terrors, is a strong foe. When our souls are departing, there is no cordial like the strong wine of assurance.

2. Assurance is to be desired, because it tends to make a Christian an active working Christian. None, generally speaking, do so much for Christ on earth as those who enjoy the fullest confidence of a free entrance into heaven, and trust not in their own works but in the finished work of Christ. That sounds astonishing, I dare say – but it is true.

A believer who lacks an assured hope will spend much of his time in inward searchings of heart about his own state. Like a nervous hypochondriac person, he will be full of his own ailments, his own doubtings and questionings, his own conflicts and corruptions. In short, you will often find he is so taken up with his internal warfare that he has little leisure for other things and little time to work for God.

But a believer who has, like Paul, an assured hope, is free from these harassing distractions. He does not vex his soul with doubts about his own pardon and acceptance. He looks at the everlasting covenant sealed with blood, at the finished work and never-broken word of his Lord and Saviour – and therefore counts his salvation a settled thing. And thus he is able to give an undivided attention to the work of the Lord and so in the long run to do more.

Take, for an illustration of this, two English emigrants, and suppose them set down side by side in New Zealand or Australia. Give each of them a piece of land to clear and cultivate. Let the portions allotted to them be the same, both in quantity and quality. Secure that land to them by every needful legal instrument; let it be conveyed as freehold to them and theirs forever; let the conveyance be publicly registered and the property made sure to them by every deed and security that man's ingenuity can devise.

Suppose then that one of them shall set to work to clear his land and bring it into cultivation and labour at it day after day without intermission or cessation.

Suppose in the meanwhile that the other shall be continually leaving his work and going repeatedly to the public registry to ask whether the land really is his own, whether there is not some mistake, whether after all there is not some flaw in the legal instruments which conveyed it to him.

The one shall never doubt his title, but just work diligently on. The other shall hardly ever feel sure of his title, and spend half his time in going to Sydney or Melbourne or Auckland with needless inquiries about it.

Which now of these two men will have made most progress in a year's time? Who will have done the most for his land, got the greatest breadth of soil under tillage, have the best crops to show, be altogether the most prosperous?

Anyone of common sense can answer that question. I need not supply an answer. There can be only one reply. *Undivided attention will always attain the greatest success.*

It is much the same in the matter of our title to 'mansions in the skies'. None will do so much for the Lord who bought him as the believer who sees his title clear and is not distracted by unbelieving doubts, questionings and hesitations. The joy of the Lord will be that man's strength. 'Restore to me,' says David, 'the joy of your salvation ... Then I will teach transgressors your ways' (Ps. 51:12,13).

Never were there such working Christians as the apostles. They seemed to live to labour. Christ's work was truly their food and drink. They counted not their lives dear to themselves. They spent, and were spent. They laid down ease, health, worldly comfort – at the foot of the cross. And one grand cause of this, I believe, was their assured hope. They were men who could say, 'We *know* that we are children of God, and that the whole world is under the control of the evil one' (1 John 5:19, italics mine).

3. Assurance is to be desired, because it tends to make a Christian a *decided* Christian. Indecision and doubt about our own state in God's sight is a grievous evil, and the mother of many evils. It often produces a wavering and unstable walk in following the Lord. Assurance helps to cut many a knot, and to make the path of Christian duty clear and plain.

Many, of whom we feel hopes that they are God's children, and have true grace, however weak, are continually perplexed with doubts on points of practice. 'Should we do such and such a thing? Shall we give up this family custom? Ought we to go into that company? How shall we draw the line about friendships? What is to be the measure of our dressing and our entertainments? Are we never, under any circumstances, to dance, never to touch a card, never to attend parties of pleasure?' These are the kind of questions which seem to give them constant trouble. And often, very often, the simple root of their perplexity is that they do not feel assured they are themselves children of God. They have not yet settled the point which side of the gate they are on. They do not know whether they are inside the ark, or not!

That a child of God ought to act in a certain decided way, they quite feel; but the grand question is, 'Are they children of God themselves?' If they only felt they were so, they would go straight forward and take a decided line. But not feeling sure about it, their conscience is forever hesitating and coming to a deadlock. The devil whispers, 'Perhaps, after all, you are only a hypocrite – what right have you to take a decided course? Wait until you are really a Christian.' And this whisper too often turns the scale and leads on to some miserable compromise or wretched conformity to the world!

I believe we have here one chief reason why so many in this day are inconsistent, trimming, unsatisfactory and half-hearted in their conduct about the world. They feel no assurance that they are Christ's, and so feel a hesitancy about breaking with the world. They shrink from laying aside all the ways of the old man because they are not quite confident they have put on the new. In short, I have little doubt that one secret cause of 'halting between two opinions' is lack of assurance. When people can say decidedly, 'The LORD – he is God!', their course becomes very clear (1 Kgs. 18:39).

4. Assurance is to be desired, because it tends to make the *holiest* Christians. This, too, sounds incredible and strange – and yet it is true. It is one of the paradoxes of the gospel, contrary at first sight to reason and common sense, and yet it is a fact. Cardinal Bellarmine was seldom more wide of the truth than when he said, 'Assurance tends to carelessness and sloth.' He who is freely forgiven by Christ will always do much for Christ's glory; and he who enjoys the fullest assurance of this forgiveness will ordinarily keep up the closest walk with God. It is a faithful saying and worthy to be remembered by all believers: 'All who have this hope in him *purify* themselves, just as he is pure' (1 John 3:3, italics mine). A hope that does not purify is a mockery, a delusion and a snare.

None are so likely to maintain a watchful guard over their own hearts and lives as those who know the comfort of living in close communion with God. They feel their privilege and will fear losing it. They will dread falling from the high estate, and marring their own comforts, by bringing clouds between themselves and Christ. He who goes on a journey with little money takes little thought of danger and cares little how late he travels. He, on the contrary, that carries gold and jewels will be a cautious traveller. He will look well to his roads, his lodgings and his company, and run no risks. It is an old saying, however unscientific it may be, that the fixed stars are those which tremble most. The man that most fully enjoys the light of God's reconciled countenance will be a man tremblingly afraid of losing its blessed consolations and jealously fearful of doing anything to grieve the Holy Spirit.

I commend these four points to the serious consideration of all professing Christians. Would you like to feel the everlasting arms around you, and to hear the voice of Jesus daily drawing near to your soul and saying, 'I am your salvation'? Would you like to be a useful labourer in the vineyard in your day and generation? Would you be known of all men as a bold, firm, decided, single-eyed, uncompromising follower of Christ? Would you be eminently spiritually minded and holy? I doubt not some readers will say, 'These are the very things our hearts desire! We long for them. We pant after them – but they seem far from us.'

Now, has it never struck you that your neglect of assurance may possibly be the main secret of all your failures, that the low measure of faith which satisfies you may be the cause of your low degree of peace? Can you think it a strange thing that your graces are faint and languishing, when faith, the root and mother of them all, is allowed to remain feeble and weak?

Take my advice this day. Seek an increase of faith. Seek an assured hope of salvation like the apostle Paul's. Seek to obtain a simple, childlike confidence in God's promises. Seek to be able to say with Paul, 'I *know* whom I have believed! I am persuaded that He is mine, and I am His!'

You have very likely tried other ways and methods – and completely failed. Change your plan. Go upon another tack. Lay aside your doubts. Lean more entirely on the Lord's arm. Begin with implicit trusting. Cast aside your faithless backwardness to take the Lord at His word. Come and roll yourself, your soul and your sins, upon your gracious Saviour. Begin with simple believing, and all other things shall soon be added to you.

Some probable causes why an assured hope is so seldom attained

This is a very serious question and ought to raise in all of us great searchings of heart. Few, certainly, of Christ's people seem to reach up to this blessed spirit of assurance. Many comparatively believe – but few are fully persuaded. Many comparatively have saving faith – but few that glorious confidence which shines forth in the language of Paul. That such is the case, I think we must all allow.

Now, why is this so? Why is a thing which two apostles have strongly enjoined us to seek after a thing of which few believers have any experimental knowledge in these latter days? *Why is an assured hope so rare?*

I desire to offer a few suggestions on this point, with all humility. I know that many have never attained assurance, at whose feet I would gladly sit both in earth and heaven. Perhaps the Lord sees something in the natural temperament of some of His children which makes assurance unwholesome for them. Perhaps, in order to be kept in spiritual health, they need to be *kept very low*. God only knows. Still, after every allowance, I fear there are many believers without an assured hope, whose case may too often be explained by causes such as these.

1. One most common cause, I suspect, is *a defective view of the doctrine of justification.*

I am inclined to think that justification and sanctification are insensibly confused together in the minds of many believers. They receive the gospel truth, that there must be something done *in* us, as well as something done *for* us, if we are true members of Christ – and so far they are right. But then, without being aware of it, perhaps, they seem to imbibe the idea that their justification is, in some degree, affected by something within themselves. They do not clearly see that Christ's work, not their own work – either in whole or in part, either directly or indirectly – is the only ground of our acceptance with God: that justification is a thing entirely outside of us, for which nothing whatever is needful on our part but simple faith, and that the weakest believer is as fully and completely justified as the strongest.

Many appear to forget that we are saved and justified as sinners, and only sinners, and that we never can attain to anything higher, if we live to the age of Methuselah. *Redeemed* sinners, *justified* sinners and *renewed* sinners doubtless we must be – but sinners, sinners, sinners we shall be always to the very last!

They do not seem to comprehend that there is a wide difference between our justification and our sanctification. Our justification is a perfect finished work – and admits of no degrees. Our sanctification is imperfect and incomplete – and will be so to the last hour of our life. They appear to expect that a believer may at some period of his life be in a measure free from corruption, and attain to a kind of inward perfection. And not finding this angelic state of things in their own hearts they at once conclude there must be something very wrong in their state. And so they go mourning all their days, oppressed with fears that they have no part or lot in Christ, and refusing to be comforted.

Let us weigh this point well. If any believing soul desires assurance and has not got it, let him ask himself, first of all, if he is quite sure he is sound in the faith, if he knows how to distinguish things that differ and if his eyes are thoroughly clear in the matter of justification. He must know what it is simply to believe and to be justified by faith, before he can expect to feel assured.

In this matter, as well as in many others, the old Galatian heresy is the most fertile source of error, both in doctrine and in practice. People ought to seek clearer views of Christ and what Christ has done for them. Happy is the man who really understands 'justification by faith – without the deeds of the law'.

2. Another common cause of the absence of assurance is _slothfulness about growth in grace._

I suspect many true believers hold dangerous and unscriptural views on this point; I do not, of course, mean intentionally – but they do hold them. Many appear to think that once converted they have little more to attend to, and that a state of salvation is a kind of easy chair in which they may just sit still, lie back and be happy. They seem to imagine that grace is given to them that they may enjoy it; and they forget that it is given, like a talent, to be used, employed and improved. Such people lose sight of the many direct injunctions to increase, to grow, to abound more and more, to add to our faith and the like; and in this little-doing condition, this sitting-still state of mind, I never marvel that they miss assurance.

I believe it ought to be our continual aim and desire to _go forward_, and our watchword on every returning birthday and at the beginning of every year should be 'more and more' (1 Thess. 4:1) – more knowledge, more faith, more obedience, more love. If we have brought forth thirty-fold, we should seek to bring forth sixty; and if we have brought forth sixty, we should strive to bring forth a hundred. The will of the Lord is our sanctification, and it ought to be our will too (Matt. 13:23; 1 Thess. 4:3).

One thing, at all events, we may depend upon – _there is an inseparable connection between diligence and assurance._ '... make every effort,' says Peter, 'to confirm your calling and election' (2 Pet. 1:10); 'We want each of you,' says Paul, 'to show this same diligence to the very end, so that what you hope for may be fully realized' (Heb. 6:11); '... the desires of the diligent,' says Solomon, 'are fully satisfied' (Prov. 13:4). There is much truth in the old maxim of the

Puritans: 'Saving faith comes by hearing – but faith of assurance comes not without doing.'

Is any reader of this message one of those who desire assurance, but have not got it? Mark my words. You will never get it without diligence, however much you may desire it. There are *no gains without pains* in spiritual things, any more than in temporal things. 'A *sluggard*'s appetite is never filled' (Prov. 13:4, italics mine).

3. Another common cause of a lack of assurance is *an inconsistent walk in life.*

With grief and sorrow, I feel constrained to say that I fear nothing more frequently prevents men attaining an assured hope than this. The stream of professing Christianity in this day is far wider than it formerly was, and I am afraid we must admit at the same time that it is much more shallow.

Inconsistency of life is utterly destructive of peace of conscience! The two things are incompatible! They cannot and they will not go together. If you will have your besetting sins and cannot make up your minds to give them up, if you will shrink from cutting off the right hand and plucking out the right eye when occasion requires it, you will have no true assurance.

A vacillating walk,

a backwardness to take a bold and decided line,

a readiness to conform to the world,

a hesitating witness for Christ,

a lingering tone of religion,

a clinching from a high standard of holiness and spiritual life –

all these make up *a sure receipt for bringing a blight upon the garden of your soul*!

It is vain to suppose you will feel assured and persuaded of your own pardon and acceptance with God unless you count all God's commandments concerning all things to be right, and hate every sin, whether great or small (Ps. 119:128). One Achan allowed in the camp of your heart will weaken your hands and lay your consolations low in the dust. You must be daily sowing to the Spirit if you are to reap the witness of the Spirit. You will not find and feel that all the Lord's ways are ways of pleasantness unless you labour in all your ways to please the Lord.

I bless God that our salvation in no way depends on our own works. By grace we are saved – not by works of righteousness – through faith, without the deeds of the law. But I never would have any believer for a moment forget that our *sense of salvation* depends much on the manner of our living. Inconsistency will dim our eyes and bring clouds between us and the sun. The sun is the same behind the clouds, but you will not be able to see its brightness or enjoy its warmth; and your soul will be gloomy and cold. It is in the path of well-doing that the dayspring of assurance will visit you and shine down upon your heart.

'The Lord confides,' says David, 'in those who fear him; he makes his covenant known to them' (Ps. 25:14).

'... to the blameless I will show my salvation' (Ps. 50:23).

'Great peace have those who love your law, and nothing can make them stumble' (Ps. 119:165).

'... if we walk in the light, as he is in the light, we have fellowship with one another' (1 John 1:7).

'... let us not love with words or speech but with actions and in truth. This is how we know that we belong to the truth and how we set our hearts at rest in his presence' (1 John 3:18,19).

'We know that we have come to know him if we keep his commands' (1 John 2:3).

Paul was a man who exercised himself to have always a conscience void of offence towards God and towards man (Acts 24:16). He could say with boldness, 'I have fought the good fight ... I have kept the faith.' I do not therefore wonder that the Lord enabled him to add with confidence, 'Now there is in store for me the crown of righteousness, which the Lord ... will award to me on that day' (2 Tim. 4:7,8).

If any believer in the Lord Jesus desires assurance and has not got it, let him think over this point also. Let him look at his own *heart*, look at his own *conscience*, look at his own *life*, look at his own *ways*, look at his own *home*. And perhaps when he has done that, he will be able to say, 'There is a cause why I have no assured hope.'

I leave the three matters I have just mentioned to the private consideration of every reader of this message. I am sure they are worth examining. May we examine them honestly. And may the Lord give us understanding in all things.

1. And now in closing this important inquiry, let me speak first to those readers who have not yet given themselves to the Lord, who have not yet come out from the world, chosen the good part and followed Christ. I ask you, then, to learn from this subject the privileges and comforts of a true Christian.

I would not have you judge of the Lord Jesus Christ by His

people. The best of servants can give you but a faint idea of that glorious Master. Neither would I have you judge of the privileges of His kingdom by the measure of comfort to which many of His people attain. Alas, we are most of us poor creatures! We come short, very short, of the blessedness we might enjoy. But, depend upon it, there are glorious things in the city of our God, which those who have an assured hope taste, even in their lifetime. There are lengths and breadths of peace and consolation there which it has not entered into your heart to conceive. There is bread enough and to spare in our Father's house, though many of us certainly eat but little of it, and continue weak. But the fault must not be laid to our Master's charge – it is all our own.

And, after all, the weakest child of God has a mine of comforts within him, of which you know nothing. You see the conflicts and tossings of the surface of his heart, but you see not the pearls of great price which are hidden in the depths below. The feeblest member of Christ would not change conditions with you! The believer who possesses the least assurance is far better off than you are. He has a *hope*, however faint – but you have none at all. He has ...

a *portion* that will never be taken from him,

a *Saviour* that will never forsake him,

a *treasure* that fades not away –

however little he may realize it all at present. But as for you, if you die as you are, your vain expectations will all perish. Oh, that you were wise! Oh, that you understood these things! Oh, that you would consider your latter end!

I feel deeply for you in these latter days of the world, if I ever did. I feel deeply for those whose treasure is all on earth, and whose hopes are all on this side of the grave. Yes! When I see old kingdoms and dynasties shaking to the very foundation; when I see, as we all saw a few years ago, kings and princes and rich men and great men fleeing for their lives and scarcely knowing where to hide their heads; when I see property dependent on public confidence melting like snow in spring, and public stocks and funds losing their value – when I see these things I feel deeply for those who have no better portion than this world can give them, and no place in that kingdom which cannot be removed.

Take advice of a minister of Christ this very day. Seek *durable riches*, a *treasure* that cannot be taken from you, a *city* which has lasting foundations. Do as the apostle Paul did. Give yourself to the Lord Jesus Christ, and seek that incorruptible crown He is ready to bestow. Take His yoke upon you, and learn of Him. Come away from a world which will never really satisfy you, and from sin which will bite like a serpent, if you cleave to it, at last. Come to the Lord Jesus as lowly sinners, and He will receive you, pardon you, give you His renewing Spirit, fill you with peace. This shall give you more real comfort than the world has ever done. There is a *gulf in your heart* which nothing but the peace of Christ can fill. Enter in and share our privileges. Come with us, and sit down by our side.

2. Lastly, let me turn to all *believers* who read these pages and speak to them a few words of brotherly counsel.

The main thing that I urge upon you is this: if you have not got an assured hope of your own acceptance in Christ, resolve this day to seek it. Labour for it. Strive after it. Pray for it. Give the Lord no rest until you 'know whom you have believed'.

I feel, indeed, that the small amount of assurance in this day, among those who are reckoned God's children, is a shame and a reproach. 'It is a thing to be heavily bewailed,' says old Traill, 'that many Christians have lived twenty or forty years since Christ called them by His grace – yet remain doubting.' Let us call to mind the earnest 'desire' Paul expresses that 'every one' of the Hebrews should seek after full assurance; and let us endeavour, by God's blessing, to roll this reproach away (Heb. 6:11, KJV).

Believing reader, do you really mean to say that you have no desire to exchange ...

hope – for *confidence*,

trust – for *persuasion*,

uncertainty – for *knowledge*?

Because weak faith will save you, will you therefore rest content with it? Because assurance is not essential to your entrance into heaven, will you therefore be satisfied without it upon earth? Alas, this is not a healthy state of soul to be in; this is not the mind of the apostolic day! Arise at once and go forward. Do not stay at the *elementals* of religion – go on to *maturity*. Do not be content with a day of small things. Never despise it in others, but never be content with it yourself.

Believe me, believe me, assurance is worth the seeking. You forsake your own mercies when you rest content without it. The things I speak are for your peace. If it is good to be sure in earthly things, then how much better is it to be sure in heavenly things! Your salvation is a fixed and certain thing. God knows it. Why should not you seek to know it too? There is nothing unscriptural in this. Paul never saw the book of life, and yet Paul says, 'I *know* and am *persuaded*.'

Make it, then, your daily prayer, that you may have an increase of faith. According to your faith will be your peace. Cultivate that blessed *root* more, and sooner or later, by God's blessing, you may hope to have the *flower*. You may not perhaps attain to full assurance all at once. It is good sometimes to be kept waiting: we do not value things which we get without trouble. But though it tarries, wait for it. Seek on, and expect to find.

There is one thing, however, of which I would not have you ignorant: you must not be surprised if you have occasional doubts after you have assurance. You must not forget you are on earth and not yet in heaven. You are still in the body and have *indwelling sin* – the flesh will lust against the spirit to the very end. The leprosy will never be out of the walls of the old house until death takes it down. And there is a *devil*, too, and a strong devil – a devil who tempted the Lord Jesus, and gave Peter a fall, and he will molest you as well. Some doubts there always will be. He who never doubts has nothing to lose. He who never fears possesses nothing truly valuable. He who is never jealous knows little of deep love. But be not discouraged: you shall be more than conqueror through Him that loved you.

Finally, do not forget that *assurance is a thing which may be lost for a season* even by the brightest Christians, unless they take care.

Assurance is a most delicate plant. It needs daily, hourly watching, watering, tending, cherishing. So watch and pray the more when you have got it. As Rutherford says, 'Make much of assurance.' Be always upon your guard. When Christian slept in the arbour, in *The Pilgrim's Progress*, he lost his certificate. Keep that in mind.

David lost assurance for many months by falling into transgression. Peter lost it when he denied his Lord. Each found it again undoubtedly, but not until after bitter tears. Spiritual darkness comes on horseback and goes away on foot! It is upon us before we know that it is coming. It leaves us slowly, gradually, and not until after many days. It is easy to run downhill. It is hard work to climb uphill. So remember my caution – when you have the joy of the Lord, watch and pray.

Above all, *grieve* not the Spirit. *Quench* not the Spirit. *Vex* not the Spirit. Drive Him not to a distance, by *tampering with small bad habits and little sins*. Little jarrings between husbands and wives make unhappy homes, and petty inconsistencies, known and allowed, will bring in a strangeness between you and the Spirit.

Hear the conclusion of the whole matter. The man who walks with God in Christ most closely will generally be kept in the greatest peace.

The believer who follows the Lord most fully and aims at the highest degree of holiness will ordinarily enjoy the most assured hope and have the clearest persuasion of his own salvation!

8

Christ's Greatest Trophy

'One of the criminals who hung there
hurled insults at him: "Aren't you the
Messiah? Save yourself and us!"
But the other criminal rebuked him. "Don't
you fear God," he said, "since you are under
the same sentence? We are punished justly,
for we are getting what our deeds deserve.
But this man has done nothing wrong."
Then he said, "Jesus, remember me when
you come into your kingdom."

Jesus answered him, "Truly I tell you, today you will be with me in paradise."'

(Luke 23:39–43)

There are few passages in the New Testament which are more familiar to men's ears than the verses which head this message. They contain the well-known story of 'the penitent thief'.

And it is right and good that these verses should be well known.

They have *comforted* many troubled minds;

they have brought *peace* to many uneasy consciences;

they have been a *healing balm* to many wounded hearts;

they have been a *medicine* to many sin-sick souls;

they have *smoothed* down not a few dying pillows.

Wherever the gospel of Christ is preached, they will always be honoured, loved and had in remembrance.

I wish to say something about these verses. I will try to unfold the leading lessons which they are meant to teach. I cannot see the peculiar mental state of anyone into whose hands this message may fall. But I can see truths in this passage which no man can ever know too well. Here is the greatest trophy which Christ ever won!

First of all, we learn from these verses –

1. Christ's power and willingness to save sinners

This is the main doctrine to be gathered from the history of the penitent thief. It teaches us that which ought to be music in the ears of all who hear it – it teaches us that Jesus Christ is 'mighty to save' (Isa. 63:1).

I ask anyone to say whether a case could look more hopeless and desperate than that of this penitent thief once did.

He was a wicked man, a malefactor, a thief, if not a murderer. We know this, for such only were crucified. He was suffering a just punishment for breaking the laws. And as he had lived wicked so he seemed determined to die wicked, for at first, when he was crucified, he railed on our Lord.

And he was a dying man. He hung there, nailed to a cross, from which he was never to come down alive. He had no longer power to stir hand or foot. His hours were numbered; the grave was ready for him. There was but a step between him and death.

If ever there was a soul hovering on the brink of hell, it was the soul of this thief! If ever there was a case that seemed lost, gone and past recovery, it was his. If ever there was a man whom the devil made sure of as his own, it was this man.

But see now what happened. He ceased to rail and blaspheme, as he had done at the first; he began to speak in another manner altogether. He turned to our blessed Lord in *prayer*. He prayed Jesus to remember him when He came into His kingdom. He asked that his soul might be cared for, his sins pardoned and himself thought of in another world. Truly this was a wonderful change!

And then mark what kind of *answer* he received. Some would have said that he was too wicked a man to be saved – but it was not so. Some would have imagined that it was too late, that the door was shut, and that there was no room for mercy; but it proved not too late at all. The Lord Jesus ...

returned him an immediate answer,

spoke kindly to him,

assured him that he would be with Him that day in paradise,

pardoned him completely,

cleansed him thoroughly from his sins,

received him graciously,

justified him freely,

raised him from the gates of hell,

gave him a title to glory.

Of all the multitude of saved souls none ever received so glorious an assurance of his own salvation as did this penitent thief. Go over the whole list, from Genesis to Revelation, and you will find none who had such words spoken to him as these: '... today *you* will be with me in paradise.'

I believe the Lord Jesus never gave so complete a proof of His power and will to save as He did upon this occasion. In the day when He seemed most weak, He showed that He was a strong deliverer. In the hour when His body was racked with pain, He showed that He could feel tenderly for others. At the time when He Himself was dying, He conferred on a sinner eternal life.

Now, have I not a right to say, Christ 'is able to save completely those who come to God through him' (Heb. 7:25)? Behold the proof of it. If ever a sinner was too far gone to be saved, it was this thief. Yet he was plucked as a brand from the fire!

Have I not a right to say, 'Christ will receive *any* poor sinner who comes to Him with the prayer of faith, and cast out none!' Behold the proof of it. If ever there was one who seemed too bad to be received, this was the man. Yet the door of mercy was wide open even for him.

Have I not a right to say, 'By grace you may be saved through faith, not of works. Fear not, only believe.' Behold the proof of it.

This thief was never baptized;

he belonged to no visible church;

he never received the Lord's Supper;

he never did any work for Christ;

he never gave money to Christ's cause.

But he had *faith* – and so he was saved!

Have I not a right to say, 'The youngest faith will save a man's soul, if it only is true? Behold the proof of it. This man's faith was only one day old, but it led him to Christ, and preserved him from hell.'

Why then should any man or woman despair, with such a passage as this in the Bible? Jesus is a Physician who can *cure hopeless cases*. He can *quicken dead souls*.

Never should any man or woman despair! Jesus is still the same now as He was 1,800 years ago. The keys of death and hell are in His hand. When He opens none can shut.

What though your sins are more in number than the hairs of your head? What though your evil habits have grown with your growth, and strengthened with your strength? What though you have hitherto hated good and loved evil all the days of your life? These things are sad indeed, but there is hope, even for you. Christ can heal you, Christ can raise you from your low estate. Heaven is not shut against you. Christ is able to admit you, if you will humbly commit your soul into His hands.

Are your sins forgiven? If not, I set before you this day a full and free salvation. I invite you to follow the steps of the penitent thief – come to Christ and live. I tell you that Jesus is full of pity, and of tender mercy. I tell you He can do everything that your soul requires. Though your sins be as scarlet, He can make them as white as snow;

though they are red like crimson, they shall be as wool. Why should you not be saved, as well as another? Come unto Christ and live.

Are you a true believer? If you are, you ought to glory in Christ. Do not glory in your own faith, your own feelings, your own knowledge, your own prayers, your own amendment, your own diligence. Glory in nothing but Christ. Alas! The best of us know but little of that merciful and mighty Saviour. We do not exalt Him and glory in Him enough. Let us pray that we may see more of the fullness that there is in Him.

Do you ever try to do good to others? If you do, remember to tell them about Christ. Tell the young, tell the poor, tell the aged, tell the ignorant, tell the sick, tell the dying – tell them all about Christ. Tell them of His power, and tell them of His love; tell them of His doings, and tell them of His feelings; tell them what He has done for the chief of sinners; tell them what He is willing to do to the last day of time; tell it them over and over again. Never be tired of speaking of Christ. Say to them broadly and fully, freely and unconditionally, unreservedly and undoubtingly: 'Come unto Christ, as the penitent thief did; come unto Christ, and you shall be saved.'

Secondly, we learn from these verses –

2. If some are saved in the very hour of death, others are not

This is a truth that never ought to be passed over, and I dare not leave it unnoticed. It is a truth that stands out plainly in the sad end of the *other* malefactor, and is only too often forgotten. Men forget that there were *two* thieves.

What became of the other thief who was crucified? Why did he not turn from his sin, and call upon the Lord? Why did he remain hardened and impenitent? Why was he not saved? It is useless to try to answer such questions. Let us be content to take the fact as we find it, and see what it is meant to teach us.

We have no right whatever to say this thief was a worse man than his companion, as there is nothing to prove it.

Both plainly were wicked men;

both were receiving the due reward of their deeds;

both hung by the side of our Lord Jesus Christ;

both heard Him pray for His murderers;

both saw Him suffer patiently.

But while one repented – the other remained hardened;

while one began to pray – the other went on railing;

while one was converted in his last hours – the other died a wicked man, as he had lived;

while one was taken to paradise – the other went to his own place, the place of the devil and his angels.

Now these things are written for our warning. There is *warning* as well as *comfort* in these verses – and that is a very solemn warning, too.

They tell me loudly that though *some* may repent and be converted on their deathbeds it does not at all follow that *all* will. A deathbed is not always a *saving* time.

They tell me loudly that two men may have the same opportunities of getting good for their souls, may be placed in the same position, see the same things and hear the same things – and yet only one of the two shall take advantage of them, repent, believe and be saved.

They tell me, above all, that repentance and faith are the *gifts* of

God and are not in a man's own power, and that if any one flatters himself he can repent at his own time, choose his own season, seek the Lord when he pleases and, like the penitent thief, be saved at the very last, he may find at length he is greatly deceived.

And it is good and profitable to bear this in mind. There is an immense amount of delusion in the world on this very subject. I see many allowing life to slip away, quite unprepared to die. I see many allowing that they ought to repent, but always putting off their own repentance. And I believe one grand reason is that most men suppose they can turn to God just when they like! They wrest the parable of the labourer in the vineyard, which speaks of the eleventh hour, and use it as it never was meant to be used. They dwell on the pleasant part of the verses I am now considering, and forget the rest. They talk of the thief that went to paradise and was saved – and they forget the one who died as he had lived and was lost.

I entreat every man of common sense who reads this message to take heed that he does not fall into this mistake.

Look at the history of men in the Bible, and see how often these notions I have been speaking of are contradicted. Mark well how many proofs there are that two men may have the same light offered them, and only one use it, and that no one has a right to take liberties with God's mercy, and presume he will be able to repent just when he likes.

Look at *Saul and David*.

They lived about the same *time*;

they rose from the same *rank* in life;

they were called to the same *position* in the world;

they enjoyed the *ministry* of the same prophet, Samuel;

they *reigned* the same number of years,

Yet one was saved – and the other lost!

Look at *Sergius Paulus and Gallio.*

They were both Roman governors;

they were both wise and prudent men in their generation;

they both heard the apostle Paul preach.

But one believed and was baptized, the other 'showed no concern whatever' (Acts 18:17).

Look at the world around you. See what is going on continually under your eyes. Two sisters will often attend the same ministry, listen to the same truths, hear the same sermons, and yet only one shall be converted unto God, while the other remains totally unmoved. Two friends often read the same religious book – one is so moved by it that he gives up all for Christ; the other sees nothing at all in it, and continues the same as before. Hundreds have read Doddridge's *Rise and Progress* without profit; with Wilberforce it was one of the beginnings of spiritual life. Thousands have read Wilberforce's *Practical View of Christianity* and laid it down again unaltered from the time; Leigh Richmond read it, and he became another man. No man has any warrant for saying, 'Salvation is in my own power.'

I do not pretend to explain these things. I only put them before you as great facts, and I ask you to consider them well.

You must not misunderstand me. I do not want to discourage you. I say these things in all affection, to give you warning of danger. I do not say them to drive you back from heaven. I say them rather to draw you on, and bring you to Christ while He can be found.

I want you to beware of presumption. Do not abuse God's mercy and compassion. Do not continue in sin, I beseech you, and think you can repent and believe and be saved just when you like, when you please, when you will and when you choose. I would always set before you an open door. I would always say, 'While there is life, there is hope.' But if you would be wise, put nothing off that concerns your soul.

I want you to beware of letting good thoughts and godly convictions slip away, if you have them. Cherish them and nourish them, lest you lose them forever. Make the most of them, lest they take to themselves wings and flee away. Have you an inclination to begin praying? Put it in practice at once. Have you an idea of beginning really to serve Christ? Set about it at once. Are you enjoying any spiritual light? See that you live up to your light. Trifle not with opportunities, lest the day come when you will want to use them, and not be able. Linger not, lest you become wise too late.

You may say, perhaps, 'It is never too late to repent.' I answer, 'That is right enough; but *late repentance is seldom true*.' And I say further, you cannot be certain if you put off repenting, you will repent at all.

You may say, 'Why should I be afraid? The penitent thief was saved.' I answer, 'That is true; but look again at the passage which tells you that *the other thief was lost*.'

3. The Spirit always leads saved souls in one way

This is a point that deserves particular attention, and is often overlooked. Men look at the broad fact that the penitent thief was saved when he was dying, and they look no further.

They do not consider the *evidences* that this thief left behind him. They do not observe the abundant proof he gave of the work of the

Spirit in his heart. And these proofs I wish to trace out. I wish to show you that *the Spirit always works in one way*, and that whether He converts a man in an hour, as He did the penitent thief, or whether by slow degrees, as He does others, the steps by which He leads souls to heaven are always the same.

Let me try to make this clear to everyone who reads this message. I want to put you on your guard. I want you to shake off the common notion that there is some *easy royal road to heaven from a dying bed.* I want you thoroughly to understand that every saved soul goes through the same experience, and that the leading principles of the penitent thief's religion were just the same as those of the oldest saint that ever lived.

a) See how strong this man's *faith* was. He called Jesus 'the Messiah'. He declared his belief that He would have a 'kingdom'. He believed that He was able to give him eternal life and glory, and in this belief prayed to Him. He maintained His innocence of all the charges brought against Him. '... this man,' said he, 'has done nothing wrong.' Others perhaps may have thought the Lord innocent – none said so openly but this poor dying man.

And when did all this happen? It happened when the whole nation had denied Christ, shouting, 'Crucify him! Crucify him!' and 'We have no king but Caesar' (Luke 23:21; John 19:15) when the chief priests and Pharisees had condemned and found Him guilty of death; when even His own disciples had forsaken Him and fled; when He was hanging, faint, bleeding and dying on the cross, numbered with transgressors, and accounted accursed. This was the hour when the thief believed in Christ, and prayed to Him. Surely such faith was never seen since the world began.

The disciples had seen mighty signs and miracles. They had seen the dead raised with a word and lepers healed with a touch, the blind receiving sight, the dumb made to speak, the lame made to walk. They had seen thousands fed with a few loaves and fishes. They had seen their Master walking on the water as on dry land. They had all of them heard Him speak as no man ever spoke, and hold out promises of good things yet to come. Some of them had a foretaste of His glory in the mount of transfiguration. Doubtless their faith was 'the gift of God' but still they had much to help it.

The dying thief saw none of the things I have mentioned. He only saw our Lord in agony, and in weakness, in suffering and in pain. He saw Him undergoing a dishonourable punishment, deserted, mocked, despised, blasphemed. He saw Him rejected by all the great and wise and noble of His own people, His strength 'dried up like a potsherd', His life drawing 'near to death' (Ps. 22:15; 88:3). He saw no sceptre, no royal crown, no outward dominion, no glory, no majesty, no power, no signs of might. And yet the dying thief believed, and looked forward to Christ's kingdom.

Would you know if you have the Spirit? Then mark the question I put to you this day: where is your *faith* in Christ?

b) See what a right sense of *sin* the thief had. He says to his companion, 'We are punished justly, for we are getting what our deeds deserve.' He acknowledges his own ungodliness, and the justice of his punishment. He makes no attempt to justify himself, or excuse his wickedness. He speaks like a man humbled and self-abased by the remembrance of past iniquities. This is what all God's children feel.

They are ready to allow they are poor hell-deserving sinners. They can say with their hearts as well as with their lips, 'We have left undone the things that we ought to have done, and we have done those things that we ought not to have done, and there is no health in us.'

Would you know if you have the Spirit? Then mark my question: do you feel your sins?

c) See what *brotherly love* the thief showed to his companion.
He tried to stop his railing and blaspheming, and bring him to a better mind. 'Don't you fear God,' he says, 'since you are under the same sentence?' There is no surer mark of grace than this! Grace shakes a man out of his selfishness – and makes him feel for the souls of others. When the Samaritan woman was converted, she left her waterpot, and ran to the city, saying, 'Come, see a man who told me everything I've ever done. Could this be the Messiah?' (John 4:29). When Saul was converted, immediately he went to the synagogue at Damascus, and testified to his brethren of Israel that Christ was the Son of God (Acts 9:20).

Would you know if you have the Spirit? Then where is your charity and love to souls?

In one word, you see in the penitent thief a finished work of the Holy Spirit. Every part of the believer's character may be traced in him. As short as his life was after conversion, he found time to leave abundant evidence that he was a child of God. His faith, his prayer, his humility, his brotherly love are unmistakable witnesses of the reality of his repentance. He was not a penitent in name only – but in deed and in truth.

Let no man therefore think, because the penitent thief was saved, that men can be saved without leaving any evidence of the Spirit's work. Let such a one consider well what *evidences* this man left behind, and take care.

It is mournful to hear what people sometimes say about what they call *deathbed evidences*. It is very fearful to observe how little satisfies some people, and how easily they can persuade themselves that their friends have gone to heaven. They will tell you when their relative is dead and gone that 'he made such a beautiful prayer one day' or that 'he talked so well' or that 'he was so sorry for his old ways, and intended to live so differently if he got better' or that 'he craved nothing in this world' or that 'he liked people to read to him, and pray with him'. And because they have this to go upon, they seem to have a comfortable hope that he is saved! Christ may never have been named, the way of salvation may never have been in the least mentioned. But it matters not; there was *a little talk of religion* – and so they are content!

Now I have no desire to hurt the feelings of anyone who reads this message, but I must and will speak plainly upon this subject.

Once for all, let me say that as a general rule, *nothing is so unsatisfactory as deathbed evidences*. The things that men say, and the feelings they express when sick and frightened, are little to be depended on. Often, too often, they are the result of *fear* and do not spring from the ground of the heart. Often, too often, they are things said by rote, caught from the lips of ministers and anxious friends, but evidently not felt. And nothing can prove all this more clearly than the well-known fact that the great majority of people who make promises of amendment on a sick bed, and then for the first time talk about religion – if they recover, go back to sin and the world!

When a man has lived a life of thoughtlessness and folly, I want something more than a few fair words and good wishes to satisfy me about his soul, when he comes to his deathbed. It is not enough for me that he will let me read the Bible to him, and pray by his bedside, that he says he has 'not thought so much as he ought of religion, and he thinks he would be a different man if he got better'. All this does not content me; it does not make me feel happy about his state. It is very well as far as it goes – but it is not conversion. It is very well in its way – but it is not genuine faith in Christ. Until I see conversion, and faith in Christ, I cannot and dare not feel satisfied. Others may feel satisfied if they please, and after their friend's death say they hope he is gone to heaven. For my part, I would rather hold my tongue and say nothing. I would be content with the least measure of repentance and faith in a dying man, even though it be no bigger than a grain of mustard seed. But to be content with anything less than repentance and faith seems to me next door to infidelity.

What kind of *evidence* do you mean to leave behind as to the state of your soul? Take example by the penitent thief, and you will do well.

When we have carried you to your narrow bed, let us not have to *hunt up stray words and scraps of religion* in order to make out that you were a true believer. Let us not have to say in a hesitating way one to another, 'I trust he is happy; he talked so nicely one day, and he seemed so pleased with a chapter in the Bible on another occasion, and he liked such a person, who is a good man.' Let us be able to speak *decidedly* as to your condition. Let us have some solid proof of your *repentance*, your *faith* and your *holiness* so that none shall be able for a moment to question your state. Depend on it, without this, those you leave behind can feel no solid comfort about your soul. We may use the form of religion at your burial, and express charitable hopes. We may meet you at the churchyard gate, and say, 'Blessed are the dead who die in the Lord.' But this will not alter your condition! If you die without *conversion* to God, without *repentance* and without faith, your funeral will only be the funeral of a lost soul; you had better never have been born! We are meant, in the next place, to learn from these verses, that –

4. When believers in Christ die – they are with the Lord

This you may gather from our Lord's words to the penitent thief: '... today you will be with me in paradise.' And you have an expression very like it in the epistle to the Philippians, where Paul says he has a desire to 'depart and be with Christ' (Phil. 1:23).

I shall say but little on this subject. I would simply lay it before you, for your own private meditations. To my own mind it is very full of comfort and peace.

Believers after death are 'with Christ'. That answers many a difficult question, which otherwise might puzzle man's busy, restless mind. The abode of dead saints, their joys, their feelings, their happiness, all seem met by this simple expression – they are 'with Christ'.

I cannot enter into full explanations about the separate state of departed believers. It is a high and deep subject, such as man's mind can neither grasp nor fathom. I know their happiness falls short of what it will be when their bodies are raised again, in the resurrection at the last day, and Jesus returns to earth. Yet I know also they enjoy a blessed rest, a rest from labour, a rest from sorrow, a rest from pain

– and a rest from sin. But it does not follow because I cannot explain these things that I am not persuaded they are far happier than they ever were on earth. I see their happiness in this very passage they are 'with Christ', and when I see that I see enough.

If the sheep are with the Shepherd, if the members are with the Head, if the children of Christ's family are with Him who loved them and carried them all the days of their pilgrimage on earth, then all must be well, all must be right.

I cannot describe what kind of place paradise is, because I cannot understand the condition of a soul separate from the body. But I ask no brighter view of paradise than this – that Christ is there. All other things, in the picture which imagination draws of the state between death and resurrection, are nothing in comparison of this. How He is there, and in what way He is there, I know not. Let me only see Christ in paradise when my eyes close in death, and that suffices me. Well does the psalmist say, 'you will fill me with joy in your presence' (Ps. 16:11). It was a true saying of a dying girl, when her mother tried to comfort her by describing what paradise would be. 'There,' she said to the child, 'there you will have no pains, and no sickness; there you will see your brothers and sisters, who have gone before you, and will be always happy.' 'Ah, Mother,' was the reply, 'but there is one thing better than all, and that is, Christ will be there!'

It may be that you do not think much about your soul. It may be that you know little of Christ as your Saviour, and have never tasted by experience that He is precious. And yet perhaps you hope to go to paradise when you die. Surely this passage is one that should make you think. Paradise is a place where Christ is. Then can it be a place that you would enjoy?

It may be that you are a believer, and yet tremble at the thought of the grave. It seems cold and dreary. You feel as if all before you was dark and gloomy and comfortless. Fear not – but be encouraged by this text. You are going to paradise, and Christ will be there!

5. The eternal portion of every man's soul is close to him

'... today,' says our Lord to the penitent thief, 'today you will be with me in paradise.' He names no distant period; He does not talk of his entering into a state of happiness as a thing 'far away'. He speaks of today – 'this very day in which you are hanging on the cross'.

How near that seems! How awfully near that word brings our everlasting dwelling-place!

Happiness or misery,

sorrow or joy,

the presence of Christ or the company of devils –

all are close to us. '... there is only a step,' says David, 'between me and death' (1 Sam. 20:3). There is but a step, we may say, between ourselves and either paradise or hell.

We none of us realize this as we ought to do. It is high time to shake off the dreamy state of mind in which we live on this matter. We are apt to talk and think, even about believers, as if death was a long journey, as if the dying saint had embarked on a long voyage. It is all wrong, very wrong! Their harbour and their home is close by, and they have entered it.

Some of us know by bitter experience what a long and weary time it is between the death of those we love and the hour when we bury them out of our sight. Such weeks are the slowest, saddest, heaviest weeks in all our lives. But, blessed be God, the souls of departed saints are free from the very moment their last breath is drawn. While we are weeping, and the coffin is preparing, and the mourning being provided, and the last painful arrangements being made, the spirits of our beloved ones are enjoying the presence of Christ. They are freed forever from the burden of the flesh. They are where 'the wicked cease from turmoil, and ... the weary are at rest' (Job 3:17).

The very moment that believers die, they are in paradise. Their battle is fought; their strife is over. They have passed through that *gloomy valley* we must one day tread; they have gone over that *dark river* we must one day cross. They have drunk that *last bitter cup* which sin has mingled for man; they have reached that place where sorrow and sighing are no more. Surely we should not wish them back again. We should not weep for them – but for ourselves!

We are warring still – but they are at peace.

We are labouring – but they are at rest.

We are watching – but they are sleeping.

We are wearing our spiritual armour – but they have forever put it off.

We are still at sea – but they are safe in harbour.

We have tears – but they have joy.

We are strangers and pilgrims – but as for them, they are at home.

Surely, better are the dead in Christ than the living! Surely the very hour the poor saint dies, he is at once higher and happier than the highest upon earth.

I fear there is a vast amount of delusion on this point. I fear that many, who are not Roman Catholics, and profess not to believe in purgatory, have, notwithstanding, some strange ideas in their minds about the immediate consequences of death.

I fear that many have a sort of vague notion that there is some interval or space of time between death and their eternal state. They imagine they shall go through a kind of *purifying change*, and that though they die unfit for heaven, they shall yet be found meet for it after all!

But this is an entire mistake.

There is no change after death;

there is no conversion in the grave;

there is no new heart given after the last breath is drawn.

The very day we go, we launch forever; the day we go from this world, we begin an eternal condition. From that day there is no spiritual alteration, no spiritual change. As we die – so we shall receive our portion after death; as the tree falls – so it must lie.

If you are an *unconverted* man, this ought to make you think. Do you know you are close to hell? This very day you might die; and if you died out of Christ, you would open your eyes at once in hell, and in torment.

If you are a *true Christian*, you are far nearer heaven than you think. This very day, if the Lord should take you, you would find yourself in paradise. The good land of promise is near to you. The eyes that you closed in weakness and pain would open at once on a glorious rest, such as my tongue cannot describe.

And now let me say a few words in conclusion.

Conclusion

1. This message may fall into the hands of some humble-hearted and contrite sinner. Are you that man? Then here is encouragement for you. See what the penitent thief did, and do likewise. See how he prayed; see how he called on the Lord Jesus Christ; see what an answer of peace he obtained. Brother or sister, why should not you do the same? Why should not you also be saved?

2. This message may fall into the hands of some proud and presumptuous man of the world. Are you that man? Then take warning. See how the impenitent thief died as he had lived – and beware lest you come to a like end. Oh, erring brother or sister, be not too confident, lest you die in your sins! Seek the Lord while He may be found. Turn, turn! Why will you die?

3. This message may fall into the hands of some professing believer in Christ. Are you such a one? Then take the penitent thief's religion as a measure by which to prove your own. See that you know something of true repentance and saving faith, of real humility and fervent charity. Brother or sister, do not be satisfied with the *world's standard of Christianity*! Be of one mind with the penitent thief, and you will be wise.

4. This message may fall into the hands of someone who is mourning over departed believers. Are you such a one? Then take comfort from this Scripture. See how your beloved ones are in the best of hands. They cannot be better off. They never were so well in their lives as they are now. They are with Jesus, whom their souls loved on earth. Oh, cease from your selfish mourning! Rejoice rather that they are freed from trouble, and have entered into rest.

5. And this message may fall into the hands of some aged servant of Christ. Are you such a one? Then see from these verses how near you are to home. Your salvation is nearer than when you first believed. A few more days of labour and sorrow and the King of kings shall send for you, and in a moment your warfare shall be at end, and all shall be peace.

9

The Ruler of the Waves

'A furious squall came up, and the waves broke over the boat, so that it was nearly swamped. Jesus was in the stern, sleeping on a cushion. The disciples woke him and said to him, "Teacher, don't you care if we drown?" He got up, rebuked the wind and said to the waves, "Quiet! Be still!" Then the wind died down and it was completely calm. He said to his disciples, "Why are you so afraid? Do you still have no faith?"'

(Mark 4:37–40)

It would be well if Christians studied the four Gospels more than they do. No doubt all Scripture is profitable. It is not wise to exalt one part of the Bible at the expense of another. But I think it would be good for some who are very familiar with the epistles if they knew a little more about Matthew, Mark, Luke and John.

Now, why do I say this? I say it because I want Christians to know more about Christ. It is well to be acquainted with all the *doctrines* and *principles* of Christianity. It is better to be acquainted with *Christ Himself*. It is well to be familiar with faith and grace and justification and sanctification. They are all matters 'pertaining to the King'. But it is far better to be familiar with Jesus Himself, to see the King's own face and to behold His beauty! This is *one secret of eminent holiness*. He who would be conformed to Christ's image, and become a Christ-like man, must be constantly studying Christ Himself!

Now the Gospels were written to make us acquainted with Christ. The Holy Spirit has told us the story of His life and death, His sayings and His doings – four times over. Four different inspired hands have drawn the picture of the Saviour. His ways, His manners, His feelings, His wisdom, His grace, His patience, His love, His power are graciously unfolded to us by four different witnesses.

Ought not the *sheep* to be familiar with the Shepherd?

Ought not the *patient* to be familiar with the Physician?

Ought not the *bride* to be familiar with the Bridegroom?

Ought not the *sinner* to be familiar with the Saviour?

Beyond doubt it ought to be so. The Gospels were written to make men familiar with Christ, and therefore I wish men to study the Gospels.

On whom must we build our souls, if we would be accepted with God? We must build on the *Rock*, Christ.

From whom must we draw that grace of the Spirit which we daily need in order to be fruitful? We must draw from the *Vine*, Christ.

To whom must we look for sympathy when earthly friends fail us or die? We must look to our elder *Brother*, Christ.

By whom must our prayers be presented, if they are to be heard on high? They must be presented by our *Advocate*, Christ.

With whom do we hope to spend the eternity of glory? With the *King of kings*, Christ.

Surely we cannot know this Christ too well! Surely there is not a word, nor a deed, nor a day, nor a step, nor a thought in the record of His life which ought not to be precious to us. We should labour to be familiar with every line that is written about Jesus!

Come now, and let us study a page in our Master's history. Let us consider what we may learn from the verses of Scripture which stand at the head of this message. You there see Jesus crossing the lake of Galilee, in a boat with His disciples. You see a *sudden storm* arise while He is asleep. The waves beat into the boat and fill it. Death seems to be close at hand. The frightened disciples awake their Master and cry for help. He arises and rebukes the wind and the waves, and at once there is a calm. He mildly reproves the faithless fears of His companions, and all is over. Such is the picture. It is one full of deep instruction. Come now, and let us examine what we are meant to learn.

Following Christ will *not* prevent our having earthly sorrows and troubles

Here are the chosen disciples of the Lord Jesus in great trouble.

The faithful little flock, which believed when priests and scribes and Pharisees were all alike unbelieving, is allowed by the Shepherd to be much disturbed. The fear of death breaks in upon them like an armed man. The deep water seems likely to go over their souls. Peter, James and John, the pillars of the church about to be planted in the world, are much distressed.

Perhaps they had not reckoned on all this. Perhaps they had expected that Christ's service would at any rate lift them *above the reach of earthly trials*. Perhaps they thought that He who could raise the dead and heal the sick and feed multitudes with a few loaves and cast out devils with a word would never allow His servants to be sufferers upon earth. Perhaps they had supposed He would always grant them smooth journeys, fine weather, an easy course and freedom from trouble and care.

If the disciples thought so, they were much mistaken. The Lord Jesus taught that a man may be one of His chosen servants and yet have to go through many a trouble, and endure many a pain.

It is good to understand this clearly. It is good to understand that Christ's service never did secure a man from all the ills that flesh is heir to, and never will. If you are a believer, you must reckon on having your share ...

of sickness and pain,

of sorrow and tears,

of losses and crosses,

of deaths and bereavements,

of partings and separations,

of vexations and disappointments –

so long as you are in the body. Christ never promises that you shall get to heaven without these. He has promised that all who come to Him shall have all things pertaining to life and godliness, but He has never promised that He will make them prosperous, or rich, or healthy, and that death and sorrow shall never come to their family.

I have the privilege of being one of Christ's ambassadors. In His name I can offer eternal life to any man, woman or child who is willing to have it. In His name I offer pardon, peace, grace, glory to any son or daughter of Adam who reads this message. But I dare not offer that person worldly prosperity as part and parcel of the gospel. I dare not offer him ...

long life,

an increased income,

and freedom from pain.

I dare not promise the man who takes up the cross and follows Christ that in following Him he shall never meet with a storm.

I know well that many do not like these terms. They would prefer having ...

Christ – and good health,

Christ – and plenty of money,

Christ – and no deaths in their family,

Christ – and no wearing cares,

Christ – and a perpetual morning without clouds.

But they do not like ...

Christ – and the cross,

Christ – and tribulation,

Christ – and the conflict,

Christ – and the howling wind,

Christ – and the storm.

Is this the secret thought of anyone who is reading this message? Believe me, if it is, you are very wrong. Listen to me, and I will try to show you have yet much to learn.

How would you know who are true Christians – if following Christ was the way to be free from trouble? How would we discern the wheat from the chaff – if it were not for the winnowing of trial? How would we know whether men served Christ for His own sake or from selfish motives – if His service brought health and wealth with it as a matter of course? The winds of winter soon show us which of the trees are evergreen – and which are not. The *storms of affliction and care* are useful in the same way. They reveal whose faith is real – and whose is nothing but profession and form.

How would the great work of sanctification go on in a man, if he had no trials? Trouble is often the only *fire* which will burn away the dross that clings to our hearts. Trouble is the *pruning knife* which the great Gardener employs in order to make us fruitful in good works. The harvest of the Lord's field is seldom ripened by sunshine only. It must go through its days of *wind* and *rain* and *storm*.

If you desire to serve Christ and be saved, I entreat you to take the Lord on His own terms. Make up your mind to meet with your share of crosses and sorrows, and then you will not be surprised. For lack of understanding this, many seem to run well for a season, and then turn back in disgust, and are cast away.

If you profess to be a child of God, leave to the Lord Jesus to sanctify you in His own way. Rest satisfied that He never makes any mistakes. Be sure that He does all things well. The winds may howl around you, and waters swell. But fear not, He is leading you 'by a *straight* way to a city' where you can 'settle' (Ps. 107:7, italics mine).

Jesus Christ is truly and really Man

There are words used in this little history which, like many other passages in the Gospels, bring out this truth in a very striking way. We are told that when the waves began to break on the ship, Jesus was in the hinder part, 'sleeping on a cushion' (Mark 4:38). He was weary, and who can wonder at it, after reading the account given in the fourth chapter of Mark? After labouring all day to do good to souls, after preaching in the open air to vast multitudes, Jesus was fatigued. Surely if the sleep of the labouring man is sweet, much more sweet must have been the sleep of our blessed Lord!

Let us settle deeply in our minds this great truth that Jesus Christ was truly and indeed Man. He was equal to the Father in all things, and the eternal God. But He was also Man, and took part of flesh and blood, and was made like unto us in all things, sin only excepted. He had a body like our own. Like us, He was born of a woman. Like us, He grew and increased in stature. Like us, He was often hungry and thirsty, and faint and weary. Like us, He ate and drank, rested and slept. Like us, He sorrowed and wept and felt. It is all very astonishing – but so it is!

He who made the heavens – went to and fro as a poor weary Man on earth. He who ruled over principalities and powers in heavenly places – took on Him a frail body like our own. He who might have dwelt forever in the glory which He had with the Father, amid the praises of legions of angels – came down to earth and dwelt as a Man among sinful men. Surely this fact alone is an amazing miracle of condescension, grace, pity and love!

I find a deep mine of comfort in this thought that Jesus is perfect *Man*, no less than perfect *God*. He in whom I am told by Scripture to trust is not only a *great* High Priest – but a *compassionate* High Priest. He is not only a *powerful* Saviour – but a *sympathizing* Saviour. He is not only the Son of God, mighty to *save* – but the Son of man able to *pity*.

Who does not know that *sympathy* is one of the sweetest things left to us in this sinful world? It is one of the bright seasons in our dark journey here below, when we can find a person who enters into our troubles and goes along with us in our anxieties – who can weep when we weep, and rejoice when we rejoice.

Sympathy is far better than money, and far rarer too! Thousands can give, who know not what it is to feel. Sympathy has the greatest power to draw us, and to open our hearts. Proper and correct *counsel* often falls dead and useless on a heavy heart. Cold *advice* often makes us shut up, shrink and withdraw into ourselves, when offered in the day of trouble. But *genuine sympathy* in such a day will call out all our better feelings, if we have any, and obtain an influence over us when nothing else can. Give me the friend who, though poor in gold and silver, has always ready a sympathizing heart.

Our God knows all this well. He knows the very secrets of man's heart. He knows the ways by which that heart is most easily approached, and the springs by which that heart is most readily moved. He has wisely provided that the Saviour of the gospel should be sympathizing, as well as mighty. He has given us one who has not only a *strong hand* to pluck us as brands from the burning, but a *sympathizing heart* on which the labouring and heavy laden may find rest.

I see a marvellous proof of love and wisdom in the union of two natures in Christ's person. It was marvellous love in our Saviour to condescend to go through weakness and humiliation for our sakes, ungodly rebels as we are. It was marvellous wisdom to fit Himself in this way to be the very Friend of friends, who could not only save man, but meet him on his own ground. I want one able to perform all things needful to redeem my soul. This Jesus can do, for He is the eternal Son of God. I want one able to understand my weakness and infirmities, and to *deal gently* with my soul, while tied to a body of death. This again Jesus can do, for He was the Son of man, and had flesh and blood like my own.

Had my Saviour been *God only* – I might perhaps have trusted Him, but I never could have come near to Him without fear. Had my Saviour been *Man only* – I might have loved Him, but I never could have felt sure that He was able to take away my sins. But, blessed be God, my Saviour is God as well as Man – and Man as well as God. God, and so able to deliver me – Man, and so able to feel with me. *Almighty power* and *deepest sympathy* are met together in one glorious Person, Jesus Christ, my Lord. Surely a believer in Christ has a strong consolation. He may well trust, and not be afraid.

If any reader of this message knows what it is to go to the throne of grace for mercy and pardon, let him never forget that the Mediator by whom he draws near to God is the Man Christ Jesus.

Your soul's business is in the hand of a High Priest who can be touched with the feeling of your infirmities. You have not to do with a Being of so high and glorious a nature that your mind can in no way comprehend Him. You have to do with *Jesus*, who had a body like your own, and was a Man upon earth like yourself. He well knows that world through which you are struggling, for He dwelt in the midst of it thirty-three years. He well knows the 'opposition from sinners' which so often discourages you, for He endured it Himself (Heb. 12:3). He well knows the art and cunning of your spiritual enemy, the devil – for He wrestled with him in the wilderness. Surely with such an advocate, you may well feel bold.

If you know what it is to apply to the Lord Jesus for spiritual comfort in earthly troubles, you should well remember the days of His flesh, and His human nature.

You are applying to One who knows your *feelings* by experience, and has drunk deep of the bitter cup, for He was 'a man of suffering, and familiar with pain' (Isa. 53:3). Jesus knows the *heart* of a man, the *bodily pains* of a man, the *difficulties* of a man – for he was a Man Himself, and had flesh and blood upon earth.

He sat *wearied* by the well at Sychar.

He *wept* over the grave of Lazarus at Bethany.

He *sweat great drops of blood* at Gethsemane.

He *groaned with anguish* at Calvary.

He is no stranger to your feelings and sensations. He is acquainted with everything which belongs to human nature, sin only excepted.

a) Are you poor and needy? So also was Jesus. The foxes had holes and the birds of the air had nests – but the Son of man had nowhere to lay His head. He dwelt in a despised city. Men used to say, 'Nazareth! Can anything good come from there?' (John 1:46). He was esteemed a carpenter's son. He preached in a borrowed boat, rode into Jerusalem on a borrowed colt and was buried in a borrowed tomb.

b) Are you alone in the world, and neglected by those who ought to love you? So also was Jesus. He came unto His own, and they received Him not. He came to be a Messiah to the lost sheep of the house of Israel, and they rejected Him. The princes of this world would not acknowledge Him. The few that followed Him were publicans and fishermen. And even these at the last forsook Him, and were scattered every man to his own place.

c) Are you *misunderstood, misrepresented, slandered* and *persecuted*? So also was Jesus. He was called ...

a glutton and a drunkard,

a friend of publicans,

a Samaritan,

a madman

and a devil!

His character was belied. False charges were laid against Him. An unjust sentence was passed upon Him and, though innocent, He was condemned as a malefactor, and as such died on the cross.

d) Does Satan tempt you, and offer horrid suggestions to your mind? So also did he tempt Jesus. He bade Him to distrust God's fatherly providence: '... tell these stones to become bread.' He proposed to Him to tempt God by exposing Himself to unnecessary danger: '... throw yourself down' from the pinnacle of the temple. He suggested to Him to obtain the kingdoms of the world for His own, by one little act of submission to himself: 'All this I will give you ... if you will bow down and worship me' (Matt. 4:1–10).

e) Do you ever feel great agony and conflict of mind? Do you feel in darkness, as if God had left you? So did Jesus. Who can tell the extent of the *sufferings of mind* He went through in the garden? Who can measure the depth of His *soul's pain* when He cried, 'My God, My God, why have you forsaken me?' (Matt. 27:46).

It is impossible to conceive a Saviour more suited to the needs of man's heart than our Lord Jesus Christ, suited not only by His *power* but by His *sympathy*; suited not only by His *divinity* but by His *humanity*. Labour, I beseech you, to get firmly impressed on your mind that Christ, the refuge of souls, is Man as well as God. Honour Him as King of kings, and Lord of lords. But while you do this, never forget that He had a body, and was a Man. Grasp this truth, and never let it go. The unhappy Socinian errs fearfully when he says that Christ was only Man, and not God. But let not the rebound from that error make you forget that while Christ was very God, He was also very Man.

Listen not for a moment to the wretched argument of the Roman Catholic, when he tells you that the virgin Mary and the saints are more sympathizing than Christ. Answer him that such an argument springs from ignorance of the Scriptures and of Christ's true nature. Answer him that you have not so learned Christ as to regard Him only as an austere Judge, and a Being to be feared. Answer him that the four Gospels have taught you to regard Him as the most *loving and sympathizing of friends* – as well as the *mightiest and most powerful of saviours*. Answer him that you want no comfort from saints and angels, from the virgin Mary or from Gabriel so long as you can repose your weary soul upon the Man Christ Jesus.

There may be much weakness and infirmity – even in a true Christian

You have a striking proof of this in the conduct of the disciples here recorded when the waves broke over the ship. They awoke Jesus in haste. They said to Him, in fear and anxiety, 'Teacher, don't you care if we drown?'

There was *impatience*. They might have waited until their Lord thought fit to arise from His sleep.

There was *unbelief*. They forgot that they were in the keeping of One who had all power in His hand.

There was *distrust*. They spoke as if they doubted their Lord's care and thoughtfulness for their safety and well-being: 'Teacher, don't you care if we drown?'

Poor faithless men! What business had they to be afraid? They had seen proof upon proof that all must be well, so long as the Bridegroom was with them. They had witnessed repeated examples of His love and kindness towards them, sufficient to convince them that He would never let them come to real harm. But all was forgotten in the present danger. Sense of immediate peril often makes men have a bad memory. Fear is often unable to reason from past experience. They heard the *winds*. They saw the *waves*. They felt the *cold waters* beating over them. They imagined *death* was close at hand. They could wait no longer in suspense. 'Teacher, don't you care if we drown?'

But, after all, let us understand this is only a picture of what is constantly going on among believers in every age. There are too many disciples, I suspect, at this very day, like those who are here described.

Many of God's children get on very well, so long as they have no trials. They follow Christ very tolerably in the time of fair weather. They imagine they are trusting Him entirely. They flatter themselves they have cast every care on Him. They obtain the reputation of being very good Christians.

But suddenly some unlooked-for trial assails them.

Their *property* makes itself wings, and flies away.

Their own *health* fails.

Death comes up into their house.

Tribulation or persecution arises, because of the Word.

And where now is their faith? Where is the strong confidence they thought they had? Where is their peace, their hope, their resignation? Alas, they are sought for – and not found. They are weighed in the balances – and found wanting. Fear and doubt and distress and anxiety break in upon them like a flood, and they seem at their wits' end! I know that this is a sad description. I only put it to the conscience of every real Christian, whether it is not correct and true.

The plain truth is that there is no literal and absolute perfection among true Christians, so long as they are in the body. The best and brightest of God's saints is but a poor mixed being. Converted, renewed and sanctified though he is, he is still compassed with infirmity. There is not a just man upon earth that always does good and sins not. In *many* things, we all fall short. A man may have true saving faith – and yet not have it always close at hand and ready to be used (Eccl. 7:20; Jas. 3:2).

Abraham was the father of the faithful. By faith he forsook his country and his kindred, and went out according to the command of God to a land he had never seen. By faith he was content to dwell in the land as a stranger, believing that God would give it to him for an inheritance. And yet this very Abraham was so far overcome by unbelief that he allowed Sarah to be called his sister, and not his wife, through the fear of man. Here was great infirmity. Yet there have been few greater saints than Abraham.

David was a man after God's own heart. He had faith to go out to battle with the giant Goliath when he was but a youth. He publicly declared his belief that the Lord, who delivered him from the paw of the lion and bear, would deliver him from this Philistine. He had faith to believe God's promise that he should one day be King of Israel, though he was owned by a few followers, though Saul pursued him like a partridge on the mountains, and there often seemed but a step between him and death. And yet this very David at one time was so far overtaken by fear and unbelief that he said, 'One of these days I shall be destroyed by the hand of Saul' (1 Sam. 27:1). He forgot the many wonderful deliverances he had experienced at God's hand. He only thought of his present danger, and took refuge among the ungodly Philistines. Surely here was great infirmity. Yet there have been few stronger believers than David.

I know it is easy for a man to reply, 'All this is very true – but it does not excuse the fears of the disciples. They had Jesus actually with them. They ought not to have been afraid. I would never have been so cowardly and faithless as they were!' I tell the man who argues in that way that he knows little of his own heart. I tell him no one knows the length and breadth of his own infirmities. No one can say how much *weakness* might appear in himself if he was placed in circumstances to call it forth.

Does any reader of this message think that he believes in Christ? Do you feel such love and confidence in Him that you cannot understand being greatly moved by any event that could happen? It is all well. I am glad to hear it. But has this faith been tried? Has this confidence been put to the test? If not, take heed of condemning these disciples hastily. Be not high-minded – but fear. Do not think because your heart is in a lively frame now that such a frame will always last. Say not, because your feelings are warm and fervent today, 'Tomorrow shall be as today, and much more abundant.' Say not, because your heart is lifted up just now with a strong sense of Christ's mercy, 'I shall never forget Him as long as I live.'

Oh, learn to abate something of this flattering estimate of yourself. You do not know yourself thoroughly. There are more things in your inward man than you are at present aware of. The Lord may leave you as He did Hezekiah to show you all that is in your heart (2 Chr. 32:31). Blessed is they that 'clothe yourselves with humility'; 'Blessed is the one who always trembles before God'; '... if you think you are standing firm, be careful that you don't fall!' (1 Pet. 5:5; Prov. 28:14; 1 Cor. 10:12).

Why do I dwell on this? Do I want to apologize for the corruptions of professing Christians, and excuse their sins? God forbid! Do I want to lower the standard of sanctification, and countenance anyone in being a lazy, idle soldier of Christ? God forbid! Do I want to wipe out the broad line of distinction between the converted and the unconverted, and to wink at inconsistencies? Once more I say, God forbid! I hold strongly that there is a mighty difference between ...

the true Christian and the false,

the believer and the unbeliever,

the children of God and the children of the world.

I hold strongly that this difference is not merely one of faith – but of life; not only one of profession – but of practice. I hold strongly that the ways of the believer should be as distinct from those of the unbeliever as ...

bitter is from sweet,

light is from darkness,

heat is from cold.

But I do want young Christians to understand what they must expect to find in themselves. I want to prevent their being stumbled and puzzled by the discovery of their own weakness and infirmity. I want them to see that they may have true faith and grace – in spite of all the devil's whispers to the contrary, though they feel within many doubts and fears. I want them to observe that Peter and James and John and their brethren were true disciples, and yet not so spiritual but that they could be afraid. I do not tell them to make the unbelief of the disciples an excuse for themselves. But I do tell them that it shows plainly that so long as they are in the body, they must not expect faith to be above the reach of fear.

Above all, I want all Christians to understand what they must expect in other believers. You must not hastily conclude that a man has no grace merely because you see some corruption in him. There are *spots* on the face of the sun – and yet the sun shines brightly and enlightens the whole world. There is *dross* mixed up with many a lump of gold that comes from Australia – and yet who thinks the gold on that account worth nothing at all? There are *flaws* in some of the finest diamonds in the world – and yet they do not prevent their being rated at a priceless value.

Away with this morbid squeamishness which makes many ready to excommunicate a man – if he only has a few faults! *Let us be quick to see grace – and more slow to see imperfections!* Let us know that if we cannot allow that there is *grace* where there is *corruption*, we shall find no grace in the world. We are yet in the body. The devil is not dead. We are not yet like the angels. Heaven has not yet begun. The leprosy is not out of the walls of the house, however much we may scrape them, and never will be until the house is taken down. Our bodies are indeed the temple of the Holy Spirit – but not a perfect temple, until they are raised or changed. Grace is indeed a treasure – but a treasure in *earthen vessels*. It is possible for a man to forsake all for Christ's sake – and yet to be overtaken occasionally with doubts and fears!

I beseech every reader of this message to remember this. It is a lesson worth attention. The apostles *believed* in Christ, *loved* Christ and *gave up all* to follow Christ. And yet you see in this storm that the apostles were afraid. Learn to be charitable in your judgement of them. Learn to be *moderate in your expectations* from your own heart. Contend to the death for the truth that no man is a true Christian who is not converted and is not a holy man. But allow that a man may be converted, have a new heart and be a holy man – and yet be liable to infirmity, doubts and fears!

The Lord Jesus Christ is *powerful*

You have a striking example of His power in the history upon which I am now dwelling. The waves were breaking into the ship where Jesus was. The terrified disciples woke Him and cried for help. 'He got up, rebuked the wind and said to the waves, "Quiet! Be still!" Then the wind died down and it was completely calm.' This was a wonderful miracle. No one could do this, but One who was almighty. The same One who spoke and brought forth the *created* universe, here reveals Himself by speaking and showing that he has *ultimate control* over it. This is power! He who has the power to bring into being matter and the seas and the wind also has the unbounded energy to harness the wind and calm the seas with a mere word, proceeding with authority from His lips.

It is good for all men to have clear views of the Lord Jesus Christ's power. Let the *sinner* know that the merciful Saviour to whom he is urged to flee and in whom he is invited to trust is nothing less than the Almighty God, and has power over all flesh to give eternal life (Rev. 1:8; John 17:2). Let the *anxious inquirer* understand that if he will only venture on Jesus, and take up the cross, he ventures on One who has all power in heaven and earth (Matt. 28:18). Let the *believer* remember as he journeys through the wilderness that his Mediator and Advocate and Physician and Shepherd and Redeemer is Lord of lords and King of kings, and that through Him all things may be done (Rev. 17:14; Phil. 4:13). Let all study the subject, for it deserves to be studied.

a) Study it in His works of *creation*. 'Through him all things were made; without him nothing was made that has been made' (John 1:3). The *heavens* and all their glorious host of inhabitants, the *earth* and all that it contains, the *sea* and all that is in it – all creation, from the sun on high to the least worm below – was the work of Christ. He *spoke* and they came into being. He *commanded* and they began to exist. That very Jesus, who was born of a poor woman at Bethlehem, and lived in a carpenter's house at Nazareth, had been the *Former* of all things. Was not this power?

b) Study it in His works of *providence*, and the orderly continuance of all things in the world. '... in him all things hold together' (Col. 1:17). Sun, moon and stars roll along in a perfect system. Spring, summer, autumn and winter follow one another in regular order. They continue to this day and fail not – according to the ordinance of Him who died on Calvary (Ps. 119:91). The *kingdoms* of this world rise and increase, and decline and pass away. The *rulers* of the earth plan and scheme and make laws and change laws and war and pull down one and raise up another. But they little think that they rule only by the will of Jesus, and that *nothing happens without the permission of the Lamb of God*. They do not know that they and their subjects are all as a drop of water in the hand of the crucified One, and that He increases the nations and diminishes the nations – just according to His mind. Is not this power?

c) Study the subject not least in the *miracles* worked by our Lord Jesus Christ during the three years of His ministry upon earth. Learn from the mighty works which He did that the things which are impossible with man are possible with Christ. Regard every one of His miracles as an emblem and figure of spiritual things. See in it a lovely picture of what He is able to do for your soul. He that could raise the dead with a word can just as easily raise man from the death of sin. He who could give sight to the blind, hearing to the deaf and speech to the dumb can also make sinners to *see* the kingdom of God, *hear* the joyful sound of the gospel, and *speak* forth the praise of redeeming love. He who could heal leprosy with a touch can heal any disease of heart. He who could cast out devils can bid every besetting sin yield to His grace. Oh, begin to read Christ's miracles in this light! As wicked and bad and corrupt as you may feel, take comfort in the thought that you are not beyond Christ's power to heal. Remember that in Christ, there is not only a fullness of *mercy* but a fullness of *power*.

d) Study the subject in particular as placed before you this day. I dare be sure your heart has sometimes been tossed to and fro like the waves in a storm. You have found it agitated like the waters of the troubled sea when it cannot rest. Come and hear this day that there is One who can give you rest. Jesus can say to your heart, whatever may be its ailment, 'Quiet, be still.'

Do you have doubts? Do you think yourself in a unique circumstance? Can Christ conquer any man's heart, even yours, and give any one rest, even you? Can He? Even if your conscience within is lashed by the recollection of countless transgressions, and torn by every gust of temptation? Even if the remembrance of past hideous immorality is grievous unto you, and the burden intolerable? Even if your heart seems full of evil, and sin appears to drag you where it will like a slave? Even if the devil rides to and fro over your soul like a conqueror, and tells you that it is vain to struggle against him, and that there is no hope for you? I tell you that here is One who can give pardon and peace to even you! My Lord and Master Jesus Christ can rebuke the devil's raging, can calm even your soul's misery, and say even to you, 'Peace, be still.' He can scatter that *cloud of guilt* which now weighs you down. He can bid *despair* to depart. He can drive *fear* away. He can remove the spirit of bondage, and fill you with the spirit of adoption. Satan may hold your soul like a strong man armed – but Jesus is stronger than he, and when He commands, the prisoners must go free. Oh, if any troubled reader wants a calm within, let him go this day to Jesus Christ, and all shall yet be well!

But what if your heart is right with God and yet you are pressed down with a *load of earthly trouble*? What if the *fear of poverty* is tossing you to and fro, and seems likely to overwhelm you? What if *pain of body* is racking you to distraction day after day? What if you are suddenly laid aside from active usefulness and compelled by infirmity to sit still and do nothing? What if death has come into your home, and taken away your Rachel or Joseph or Benjamin – and left you alone, crushed to the ground with sorrow? What if all of this has happened?

Still there is comfort in Christ. He can speak peace to wounded hearts as easily as calm troubled seas. He can rebuke rebellious wills as powerfully as raging winds. He can make storms of sorrow abate, and silence tumultuous passions as surely as He stopped the Galilean storm. He can say to the heaviest anxiety, 'Peace, be still.' The floods of care and tribulation may be mighty, but Jesus sits upon the waterfloods, and is mightier than the waves of the sea (Ps. 93:4). The winds of trouble may howl fiercely round you – but Jesus holds them in His hand, and can stay them when He desires. Oh, if any reader of this message is broken-hearted and careworn and sorrowful, let him go to Jesus Christ, and cry to Him, and he shall be refreshed. 'Come to me,' He says, 'all you who are weary and burdened, and I will give you rest' (Matt. 11:28).

I invite all who profess to call themselves Christians to take large views of Christ's power. Doubt anything else if you will – but never doubt Christ's power. Whether you do not secretly love sin may be doubtful. Whether you are not privately clinging to the world may be doubtful. Whether the pride of your nature is not rising against the idea of being saved as a poor sinner by grace may be doubtful. But one thing is not doubtful and that is, that Christ is 'able to save completely', and will save you, if you come to Him (Heb. 7:25).

Let us learn, in the last place, how tenderly and patiently the Lord Jesus deals with weak believers

We see this truth brought out in His words to His disciples, when the wind ceased and there was a calm. He might well have rebuked them sharply. He might well have reminded them of all the great things He had done for them, and reproved them for their cowardice and mistrust – but there is nothing of anger in the Lord's words. He simply asks two questions: 'Why are you so afraid? Do you still have no faith?'

The whole of our Lord's conduct towards His disciples on earth deserves close consideration. It throws a beautiful light on the compassion and patience that there is in Him. No master surely ever had scholars so slow to learn their lessons as Jesus had in the apostles. No scholars surely ever had so patient and forbearing a teacher as the apostles had in Christ. Gather up all the evidence on this subject that lies scattered through the Gospels, and see the truth of what I say.

At no time of our Lord's ministry did the disciples seem to fully comprehend the object of His coming into the world. The humiliation, the atonement, the crucifixion were hidden things to them. The plainest words and clearest warnings from their Master of what was going to befall Him seemed to have had no effect on their minds. They understood not. They perceived not. It was hidden from their eyes (Luke 9:45; 18:34). Once Peter even tried to dissuade our Lord from suffering: '"Never, Lord!" he said. "This shall never happen to you!"' (Matt. 16:22).

Frequently you will see things in their spirit and demeanour which are not at all to be commended. One day we are told they disputed among themselves who would be greatest (Mark 9:34). Another day they considered not His miracles, and their hearts were hardened (Mark 6:52). Once two of them wished to call down fire from heaven upon a village, because it did not receive them (Luke 9:54). In the garden of Gethsemane, the *three best* of them slept, when they should have watched and prayed. In the hour of His betrayal they all forsook Him and fled; and worst of all, Peter, the most forward of the twelve, denied his Master three times with an oath.

Even after the resurrection, you see the same unbelief and hardness of heart cling to them; though they saw their Lord with their eyes, and touched Him with their hands, even then some doubted. So weak were they in faith! So slow of heart were they to 'believe all that the prophets have spoken' (Luke 24:25). So backward were they in understanding the meaning of our Lord's words and actions and life and death.

But what do you see in our *Lord's behaviour* towards these disciples all through His ministry? You see nothing but unchanging pity, compassion, kindness, gentleness, patience and love. He does not cast them off for their stupidity. He does not reject them for their unbelief. He does not dismiss them forever for cowardice. He teaches them as they are able to bear. He leads them on step by step, as a nurse does an infant when it first begins to walk. He sends them kind messages as soon as He is risen from the dead. 'Go,' He said to the women, 'and tell my brothers to go to Galilee; there they will see me' (Matt. 28:10). He gathers them around Himself once more. He restores Peter to his place, and bids him, 'Feed my sheep' (John 21:17). He condescends to sojourn with them forty days before He finally ascends. He commissions them to go forth as His messengers, and preach the gospel to the Gentiles. He blesses them in parting, and encourages them with that gracious promise 'I am with you always, to the very end of the age' (Matt. 28:20). Truly this was a love that passes knowledge. This is not the manner of man.

Let all the world know that the Lord Christ is very pitiful, and of tender mercy. He will not break the bruised reed, nor quench the smoking flax. As a *father* pities his children – so He pities those who fear Him. As one whom his *mother* comforts – so will He comfort His people (Jas. 5:11; Matt. 12:20; Ps. 103:13; Isa. 66:13). He cares for the *lambs* of His flock – as well as for the old sheep. He cares for the *sick* and *feeble* ones of His fold – as well as for the strong. It is written that He will carry them in His bosom, rather than let one of them be lost (Isa. 40:11). He cares for the least member of His body, as well as for the greatest. He cares for the *babes* of His family, as well as the grown-up men. He cares for the tenderest little plants in His garden, as well as for the cedar of Lebanon. All are in His book of life, and all are under His charge. All are given to Him in an everlasting covenant, and He has undertaken, in spite of all weaknesses, to bring every one safe home. Only let a sinner lay hold on Christ by faith, and then, however feeble, Christ's word is pledged to him, 'I will never leave you nor forsake you' (see Heb. 13:5). He may *correct* him occasionally in love. He may *gently reprove* him at times. But He will never, never give him up. The devil shall never pluck him from Christ's hand!

Let all the world know that the Lord Jesus will not cast away His believing people because of shortcomings and infirmities. The husband does not put away his wife because he finds failings in her. The mother does not forsake her infant because it is weak, feeble and ignorant. And the Lord Christ does not cast off poor sinners who have committed their souls into His hands because He sees in them blemishes and imperfections. Oh, no, it is His glory ...

to pass over the faults of His people,

to heal their backslidings,

to make much of their weak graces,

and to pardon their many faults.

The eleventh of Hebrews is a wonderful chapter. It is marvellous to observe how the Holy Spirit speaks of the worthy men whose names are recorded in that chapter. The *faith* of the Lord's people is there brought forward, and held in remembrance. But the *faults* of many of them, which might easily have been brought up also, are left alone, and not mentioned at all.

Who is there now among the readers of this message that feels desires for salvation but is afraid to become decided, lest later on he should fall away? Consider, I beseech you, the tenderness and patience of the Lord Jesus, and be afraid no more. Fear not to take up the cross, and come out boldly from the world. That same Lord and Saviour who bore with the disciples, is ready and willing to bear with you.

If you *stumble*, He will raise you.

If you *err*, He will gently bring you back.

If you *faint*, He will revive you.

He will not lead you out of Egypt, and then allow you to perish in the wilderness. He will conduct you safely into the Promised Land. Only commit yourself to His guidance and then, my soul for yours, He shall carry you safely home. Only hear Christ's voice, and follow Him, and you shall never perish.

Who is there among the readers of this message that has been converted, and desires to do his Lord's will? Take as an example, this day, your Master's gentleness and long-suffering, and learn to be tender-hearted and kind to others.

Deal gently with *young beginners*. Do not expect them to know everything and understand everything all at once. Take them by the hand. Lead them on and encourage them. Believe all things and hope all things, rather than make that heart sad which God would not have made sad.

Deal gently with *backsliders*. Do not turn your back on them as if their case was hopeless. Use every lawful means to restore them to their former place. Consider yourself, and your often infirmities, and do unto others as you would be done by. Alas, there is a painful absence of the Master's mind among many of His disciples. There are few churches, I fear, in the present day, which would have received Peter into communion again for many a long year, after denying his Lord. There are few believers ready to do the work of Barnabas – willing to take young converts by the hand, and encourage them at their first beginnings. Truly we want an outpouring of the Spirit upon believers, almost as much as upon the world.

Bear with me a few moments, while I say a few words to *impress* the things you have been reading more deeply on your heart.

1. This message will very likely be read by some who know nothing of Christ's service by experience, or of Christ Himself.

There are only too many who take no interest whatever in the things about which I have been writing. Their treasure is all below. They are wholly taken up with the things of the world. They care nothing about the believer's conflict and struggles and infirmities and doubts and fears.

They care little whether Christ is Man or God. They care little whether He did miracles or not. It is all a matter of words and names and forms about which they do not trouble themselves. They are without God in the world.

If perhaps you are such a man as this, I can only warn you solemnly that your present course cannot last. You will not live forever. There must be an end. Grey hairs, old age, sickness, infirmities, death – all, all are before you, and must be met one day. What will you do when that day comes?

Remember my words this day. You will find no comfort when sick and dying unless Jesus Christ is your Friend. You will discover, to your sorrow and confusion, that however much men may talk and boast, they cannot do without Christ when they come to their deathbed. You may send for ministers, and get them to read prayers and give you the sacrament. You may go through every religious form and ceremony. But if you persist in living a careless and worldly life, and despising Christ in the morning of your days, you must not be surprised if Christ leaves you to yourself in your latter end. Alas, these are solemn words, and are often sadly fulfilled: 'I ... will laugh when disaster strikes you; I will mock when calamity overtakes you' (Prov. 1:26).

Come then, this day, and be advised by one who loves your soul. Cease to do evil. Learn to do well. Forsake the foolish, and go in the path of understanding. Cast away that pride which hangs about your heart, and seek the Lord Jesus while He may be found. Cast away that spiritual sloth which is palsying your soul, and resolve to take trouble about your Bible, your prayers and your Sundays. Break off from a world which can never really satisfy you, and seek that treasure which alone is truly incorruptible. Oh, that the Lord's own words might find a place in your conscience! 'How long will you who are simple love your simple ways? How long will mockers delight in mockery and fools hate knowledge? Repent at my rebuke!' (Prov. 1:22,23). I believe the crowning sin of Judas Iscariot was that he would not seek pardon, and turn again to his Lord. Beware lest that be your sin also.

2. This message will probably fall into the hands of some who love the Lord Jesus, and believe in Him – and yet desire to love Him better. If you are such a man, allow the word of exhortation, and apply it to your heart. Keep before your mind, as an ever-present truth, that the Lord Jesus is an actual living Person, and deal with Him as such.

I am afraid that many who profess Christ in our day have lost sight of our Lord's person. They talk ...

more about salvation – than about their only Saviour,

and more about redemption – than the one true Redeemer,

and more about Christ's work – than Christ Himself.

This is a great fault – one that accounts for the dry and shrivelled spirit that infuses the religious lives of many who profess faith.

As ever you would grow in grace, and have joy and peace in believing, beware of falling into this error. Cease to regard the gospel as a mere collection of dry doctrines. Look at it rather as the revelation of a mighty living Being in whose sight you are daily to live. Cease to regard it as a mere set of abstract propositions and abstruse principles and rules. Look at it as the introduction to a glorious personal Friend. This is the kind of gospel that the apostles preached. They did not go about the world telling men of love and mercy and pardon in the *abstract*. The leading subject of all their sermons was the loving heart of an actual living Christ. This is the kind of gospel which is most calculated to promote sanctification and fitness for glory. Nothing, surely, is so likely to prepare us for that heaven where Christ's personal presence will be all, and that glory where we shall meet Christ face to face, as to realize communion with Christ as an actual living Person here on earth. There is all the difference in the world, between an *idea* and a *person*.

Try to keep before your mind as an ever-present truth that *the Lord Jesus is utterly unchanged*. That Saviour in whom you trust is the same yesterday, today and forever. He knows no variableness, nor shadow of turning. Though high in heaven at God's right hand He is just the same in heart that He was 1,800 years ago on earth. Remember this, and you will do well.

Follow Him all through His journeys to and fro in Palestine. Mark how He received all that came to Him and cast out none. Mark how He had ...

an *ear* to listen to every tale of sorrow,

a *hand* to help every case of distress,

a *heart* to feel for all who needed sympathy.

And then say to yourself, 'This same Jesus is He who is my Lord and Saviour. Place and time have made no difference in Him. What He was, He is, and will be for evermore.'

Surely this thought will give life and reality to your daily religion. Surely this thought will give substance and shape to your expectation of good things to come. Surely it is matter for joyful reflection that He who was thirty-three years upon earth, and whose life we read in the Gospels, is the very Saviour in whose presence we shall spend eternity!

10

Christis All

'Christ is all'

(Col. 3:11)

The words of the text which heads this page are few, short and soon spoken; but they contain great things. Like those golden sayings, '... to me, to live is Christ' and 'I no longer live, but Christ lives in me', they are singularly rich and suggestive (Phil. 1:21; Gal. 2:20).

These three words are the *essence* and *substance* of Christianity. If our hearts can really go along with them, then it is well with our souls. If not, we may be sure we have yet much to learn.

Let me try to set before my readers in what sense Christ is all, and let me ask them, as they read, to judge themselves honestly that they may not make shipwreck in the judgement of the last day.

I purposely close this volume with a message on this remarkable text. Christ is the mainspring both of doctrinal and practical Christianity. A right knowledge of Christ is essential to a right knowledge of sanctification as well as justification. He who follows after holiness will make no progress unless he gives to Christ His rightful place. I began the volume with a plain statement about *sin*. Let me end it with an equally plain statement about *Christ*.

1. Christ is all in the counsels of God

a) There was a time when this earth had no being. As solid as the mountains look, as boundless as the sea appears, as high as the stars in heaven look – they once did not exist. And man, with all the high thoughts he now has of himself, was a creature unknown.

And where was Christ then?

Even then Christ was 'with God' and 'was God' and knew 'equality with God' (John 1:1; Phil. 2:6). Even then He was the beloved Son of the Father. 'You loved me,' He says, 'before the creation of the world' (John 17:24); I had 'glory ... with you before the world began' (John 17:5); 'I was formed long ages ago, at the very beginning, when the world came to be' (Prov. 8:23). Even then He was the Saviour if 'chosen before the creation of the world' (1 Pet. 1:20), and believers were 'chose[n] ... in him' (Eph. 1:4).

b) There came a time when this earth was created in its present order. Sun, moon and stars, sea, land and all their inhabitants were called into being, and made out of chaos and confusion. And, last of all, man was formed out of the dust of the ground.

And where was Christ then?

Hear what the Scripture says: 'Through him all things were made; without him nothing was made that has been made' (John 1:3); '... in him all things were created: things in heaven and on earth' (Col.

1:16); 'In the beginning, Lord, you laid the foundations of the earth, and the heavens are the work of your hands' (Heb. 1:10); 'I was there when he set the heavens in place, when he marked out the horizon on the face of the deep, when he established the clouds above and fixed securely the fountains of the deep, when he gave the sea its boundary so that the waters would not overstep his command, and when he marked out the foundations of the earth. Then I was constantly at his side' (Prov. 8:27–30). Can we wonder that the Lord Jesus, in His preaching, should continually draw lessons from the book of nature? When He spoke of the sheep, the fish, the ravens, the corn, the lilies, the fig tree, the vine, He spoke of things which He Himself had made.

c) There came a day when *sin* entered the world. Adam and Eve ate the forbidden fruit, and fell. They lost that holy nature in which they were first formed. They forfeited the friendship and favour of God and became guilty, corrupt, helpless, hopeless sinners. Sin came as a barrier between themselves and their holy Father in heaven. Had He dealt with them according to their deserts, there would have been nothing before them but death, hell and everlasting ruin.

And where was Christ then?

In that very day He was revealed to our trembling parents as the only hope of salvation. The very day they fell, they were told that the *seed of the woman* would yet bruise the serpent's head, that a Saviour born of a woman would overcome the devil, and win for sinful man an entrance to eternal life (Gen. 3:15). Christ was held up as the true light of the world, in the very day of the Fall; and never has any name been made known from that day by which souls could be saved, excepting His. By Him all saved souls have entered heaven, from Adam downwards; and without Him none have ever escaped hell.

d) There came a time when the world seemed sunk and buried in ignorance of God. After 4,000 years, the nations of the earth appeared to have clean forgotten the God who made them. Egyptian, Assyrian, Persian, Grecian and Roman empires had done nothing but spread superstition and idolatry. Poets, historians, philosophers had proved that, with all their intellectual powers, they had no right knowledge of God, and that man, left to himself, was utterly corrupt. '... the world through its wisdom did not know him' (1 Cor. 1:21). Excepting a few despised Jews in a corner of the earth, the whole world was dead in ignorance and sin.

And what did Christ do then?

He left the glory He had had from all eternity with the Father, and came down into the world to provide a salvation. He took our nature upon Him, and was born as a man. As a man He did the will of God perfectly, which we all had left undone; as a man He suffered on the cross the wrath of God, which we ought to have suffered. He brought in everlasting righteousness for us. He redeemed us from the curse of a broken law. He opened a fountain for all sin and uncleanness. He died for our sins. He rose again for our justification. He ascended to God's right hand, and there sat down, waiting until His enemies would be made His footstool. And there He sits now, offering salvation to all who will come to Him, interceding for all who believe in Him, and managing by God's appointment all that concerns the salvation of souls.

e) There is a time coming when sin shall be cast out from this world. *Wickedness* shall not always flourish unpunished,

Satan shall not always reign,

creation shall not always groan, being burdened.

There shall be a time of restitution of all things. There shall be 'a new heaven and a new earth, where righteousness dwells', and 'the earth will be filled with the knowledge of the LORD, as the waters cover the sea' (see Rom. 8:22; see Acts 3:21; 2 Pet. 3:13; Isa. 11:9).

And where shall Christ be then? And what shall He do?

Christ Himself shall be King. He shall return to this earth, and make all things new. He shall come 'on the clouds of heaven, with power and great glory', and the kingdoms of the world shall become His. The heathen shall be given to Him for His inheritance, and the uttermost parts of the earth for His possession. To Him every knee shall bow, and every tongue shall confess that He is Lord. 'His dominion is an everlasting dominion that will not pass away, and his kingdom is one that will never be destroyed' (Matt. 24:30; see Rev. 11:15; see Ps. 2:8; see Phil. 2:10,11; Dan. 7:14).

f) There is a day coming when all men shall be judged. The sea shall give up the dead who are in it, and death and hell shall deliver up the dead who are in them. All who sleep in the grave shall awake and come forth, and all shall be judged according to their works (Dan. 12:2; Rev. 20:13).

And where will Christ be then?

Christ Himself will be the Judge. The Father 'has entrusted all judgment to the Son'; 'When the Son of Man comes in his glory ... he will sit on his glorious throne. All the nations will be gathered before him, and he will separate the people one from another as a shepherd separates the sheep from the goats'; '... we must all appear before the judgment seat of Christ, so that each of us may receive what is due to us for the things done while in the body, whether good or bad' (John 5:22; Matt. 25:31,32; 2 Cor. 5:10).

Now if any reader of this message thinks little of Christ, let him know this day that he is very unlike God! You are of one mind – and God is of another. You are of one judgement – and God is of another. You think it enough to give Christ a little honour, a little reverence, a little respect. But in all the eternal counsels of God the Father, in creation, redemption, restitution and judgement – in all these, Christ is 'all'.

Surely we shall do well to consider these things. Surely it is not written in vain: 'Whoever does not honour the Son does not honour the Father, who sent him' (John 5:23).

2. Christ is all in the Bible

In every part of both Testaments Christ is to be found – dimly and indistinctly at the *beginning*, more clearly and plainly in the *middle*, fully and completely at the *end* – but really and substantially everywhere.

Christ's sacrifice and death for sinners, and Christ's kingdom and future glory, are the *light* we must bring to bear on any book of Scripture we read. Christ's *cross* and Christ's *crown* are the clue we must hold fast, if we would find our way through Scripture difficulties. Christ is the only *key* which will unlock many of the dark places of the Word. Some people complain that they do not understand the Bible. And the reason is very simple. They do not use the key. To them the Bible is like the hieroglyphics in Egypt. It is a mystery, just because they do not know and employ the key.

a) It was Christ crucified who was set forth in every Old Testament sacrifice. Every animal slain and offered on an altar was a practical confession that a Saviour was looked for who would die for sinners – a Saviour who would take away man's sin, by suffering, as his Substitute and Sin-bearer, in his stead (1 Pet. 3:18). It is absurd to suppose that an unmeaning slaughter of innocent beasts, without a distinct object in view, could please the eternal God!

b) It was Christ to whom Abel looked when he offered a better sacrifice than Cain. Not only was the heart of Abel better than that of his brother, but he showed his knowledge of vicarious sacrifice and his faith in an atonement. He offered the firstlings of his flock, with the blood thereof, and in so doing declared his belief that without shedding of blood there is no remission of sin (Heb. 11:4; Heb. 9:22).

c) It was Christ of whom Enoch prophesied in the days of abounding wickedness before the flood. 'See,' he said, 'the Lord is coming with thousands upon thousands of his holy ones to judge everyone' (Jude 14,15).

d) It was Christ to whom Abraham looked when he dwelt in tents in the land of promise. He believed that in his seed, in one born of his family, all the nations of the earth should be blessed. By faith he saw Christ's day, 'and was glad' (John 8:56).

e) It was Christ of whom Jacob spoke to his sons, as he lay dying. He marked out the tribe out of which He would be born, and foretold that gathering together unto Him which is yet to be accomplished.

'The sceptre will not depart from Judah, nor the ruler's staff from between his feet, until he to whom it belongs shall come and the obedience of the nations shall be his' (Gen. 49:10).

f) It was Christ who was the substance of the ceremonial law which God gave to Israel by the hand of Moses. The morning and evening sacrifice, the continual shedding of blood, the altar, the mercy seat, the high priest, the Passover, the day of atonement, the scapegoat – all these were so many pictures, types and emblems of Christ and His work. God had compassion upon the weakness of His people. He taught them Christ, line upon line and, as we teach little children, by similitudes. It was in this sense especially that 'the law was [a] schoolmaster' to lead the Jews 'unto Christ' (Gal. 3:24, KJV).

g) It was Christ to whom God directed the attention of Israel by all the daily miracles which were done before their eyes in the wilderness. The pillar of cloud and fire which guided them, the manna from heaven which every morning fed them, the water from the smitten rock – all and each were figures of Christ! The bronze serpent, on that memorable occasion when the plague of fiery serpents was sent upon them, was an emblem of Christ (John 3:14).

h) It was Christ of whom all the judges were types. Joshua and Gideon and Jephthah and Samson, and all the rest whom God raised up to deliver Israel from captivity – all were emblems of Christ. As weak and unstable and faulty as some of them were, they were set for examples of better things in the distant future. All were meant to remind the tribes of that far higher Deliverer who was yet to come.

i) It was Christ of whom David the king was a type. Anointed and chosen when few gave him honour, despised and rejected by Saul and all the tribes of Israel, persecuted and obliged to flee for his life, a man of sorrow all his life, and yet at length a conqueror – in all these things David represented Christ.

j) It was Christ of whom all the prophets from Isaiah to Malachi spoke. They saw through a glass darkly. They sometimes dwelt on His sufferings, and sometimes on His glory that would follow (1 Pet. 1:11). They did not always mark out for us the distinction between Christ's first coming and Christ's second coming. Like two candles in a straight line, one behind the other, they sometimes saw both of the advents at the same time, and spoke of them in one breath. They were sometimes moved by the Holy Spirit to write of the times of Christ crucified, and sometimes of Christ's kingdom in the latter days. But Jesus *dying* or Jesus *reigning* was the thought you will ever find uppermost in their minds.

k) It is Christ, I need hardly say, of whom the whole New Testament is full.

The *Gospels* are Christ living, speaking and moving among men.

The *Acts* are Christ preached, published and proclaimed.

The *epistles* are Christ written of, explained and exalted.

But all through, from first to last, there is one name above every other, and that is the name of Christ.

I charge every reader of this message to ask himself frequently what the Bible is to him. Is it a Bible in which you have found nothing more than good moral precepts and sound advice? Or is it a Bible in which you have found Christ? Is it a Bible in which Christ is all? If not, I tell you plainly, you have hitherto used your Bible to very little purpose. You are like a man who studies the solar system, and leaves out in his studies the sun, which is the centre of all. It is no wonder if you find your Bible a dull book!

3. Christ is all in the religion of all true Christians

In saying this, I wish to guard myself against being misunderstood. I hold the absolute necessity of the election of God the Father, and the sanctification of God the Spirit, in order to effect the salvation of everyone who is saved. I hold that there is a perfect harmony and unison in the action of the three Persons of the Trinity in bringing any man to glory, and that all three cooperate and work a joint work in his deliverance from sin and hell. Such as the Father is, such is the Son, and such is the Holy Spirit. The Father is merciful, the Son is merciful, the Holy Spirit is merciful. The same Three who said at the beginning, 'Let us *create*,' said also, 'let us *redeem* and *save*.' I hold that everyone who reaches heaven will ascribe all the glory of his salvation to Father, Son and Holy Spirit, three Persons in one God.

But, at the same time, I see clear proof in Scripture that it is the mind of the blessed Trinity that Christ should be prominently and distinctly exalted, in the matter of saving souls. Christ is set forth as the Word, through whom God's love to sinners is made known. Christ's incarnation and atoning death on the cross are the great *cornerstone* on which the whole plan of salvation rests. Christ is the *way* and *door* by which alone approaches to God are to be made. Christ is the *root* into which all elect sinners must be grafted. Christ is the only *meeting-place* ...

between God and man,

between heaven and earth,

between the Holy Trinity and the poor sinful child of Adam.

It is Christ whom God the Father has sealed and appointed to convey *life* to a dead world (John 6:27). It is Christ to whom the Father has given a people to be brought to glory. It is Christ of whom the Spirit testifies, and to whom He always leads a soul for pardon and peace. In short, 'God was pleased to have all his fullness dwell in him' (Col. 1:19). What the sun is in the skies of heaven – that Christ is in true Christianity.

I say these things by way of explanation. I want my readers clearly to understand that in saying, 'Christ is all', I do not mean to shut out the work of the Father and of the Spirit. Now let me show what I do mean.

a) Christ is all in a sinner's **justification** before God.

Through Him alone, we can have peace with a holy God. By Him alone, we can have admission into the presence of the Most High, and stand there without fear. 'In him and through faith in him we may approach God with freedom and confidence' (Eph. 3:12). In Him alone, can God be just, and justify the ungodly (Rom. 3:26).

With what can any mortal man come before God? What can we bring as a plea for acquittal before that glorious Being, in whose eyes the very heavens are not clean?

Shall we say that we have done our duty to God? Shall we say that we have done our duty to our neighbour? Shall we bring forward our prayers, our regularity, our morality, our amendments, our church-going? Shall we ask to be accepted with God because of any of these?

Which of these things will stand the searching inspection of God's eye? Which of them will actually justify us? Which of them will carry us clear through judgement and land us safe in glory?

None, none, none! Take any commandment of the ten, and let us examine ourselves by it. We have broken it repeatedly. We cannot answer God one of a thousand. Take any of us, and look narrowly into our ways, and we are nothing but sinners. There is but one verdict – we are all guilty, all ought to die, and all deserve hell. With which can we come before God?

We must come in the name of Jesus, standing on no other ground, pleading no other plea than this: 'Christ died on the cross for the ungodly, and I trust in Him. Christ died for me, and I believe on Him.' The garment of our Elder Brother, the righteousness of Christ, this is the only robe which can cover us and enable us to stand in the light of heaven without shame.

The name of Jesus is the only name by which we shall obtain an entrance through the gate of eternal glory. If we come to that gate in our own names we are lost, we shall not be admitted, we shall knock in vain. If we come in the name of Jesus, it is a passport and shibboleth, and we shall enter and live.

The mark of the blood of Christ is the only mark that can save us from destruction. When the angels are separating the children of Adam in the last day, if we are not found marked with that atoning blood, we had better never have been born.

Oh, let us never forget that Christ must be all to that soul who would be justified! We must be content to go to heaven as beggars, saved by free grace, simply as believers in Jesus, or we shall never be saved at all.

Is there a *thoughtless, worldly soul* among the readers of this book? Is there one who thinks to reach heaven by saying hastily at the last, 'Lord have mercy on me', without Christ? Friend, you are sowing misery for yourself, and unless you alter, you will awake to endless woe.

Is there a *proud, formal soul* among the readers of this book? Is there anyone thinking to make himself fit for heaven, and good enough to pass muster by his own doings? Brother, you are building a Babel, and you will never reach heaven in your present state.

But is there a *labouring, heavy-laden one* among the readers of this book? Is there one who wants to be saved, and feels a vile sinner? I say to such a one, 'Come to Christ, and He shall save you. Come to Christ, and cast the burden of your soul on Him. Fear not, only believe.'

Do you fear wrath? Christ can deliver you from the wrath to come.

Do you feel the curse of a broken law? Christ can redeem you from the curse of the law.

Do you feel far away? Christ has suffered, to bring you near to God.

Do you feel unclean? Christ's blood can cleanse all sin away.

Do you feel imperfect? You shall be complete in Christ.

Do you feel as if you were nothing? Christ shall be all in all to your soul.

Never did saint reach heaven with any tale but this: 'I was washed and made white in the blood of the Lamb' (see Rev. 7:14).

b) Christ is not only all in the justification of a true Christian – but He is also all in his **sanctification**. I would not have anyone misunderstand me. I do not mean for a moment to undervalue the work of the Spirit. But this I say, that no man is ever holy until he comes to Christ and is united to Him. Until then, his works are dead works, and he has no holiness at all. First you must be joined to Christ, and then you shall be holy. Without Him, separate from Him, you can do nothing (John 15:5).

And no man can grow in holiness, except he abides in Christ. Christ is the great root from which every believer must draw his strength to go forward. The Spirit is His special gift, His purchased gift for His people. Believer must not only have 'received Christ Jesus the Lord' but 'continue to live your lives in him' and be 'rooted and built up in him' (Col. 2:6,7).

Would you be holy? Then Christ is the *manna* you must daily eat, like Israel in the wilderness of old.

Would you be holy? Then Christ must be the *rock* from which you must daily drink the living water.

Would you be holy? Then you must be ever looking unto Jesus, looking at His cross, and learning fresh motives for a closer walk with God; looking at His example, and taking Him for your pattern. Looking at Him, you would become like Him. Looking at Him, your face would shine without your knowing it. Look less at *yourself*, and more at *Christ*, and you will find besetting sins dropping off and leaving you, and your eyes enlightened more and more every day (Heb. 12:2; 2 Cor. 3:18).

The true secret of coming up out of the wilderness is to come up leaning on the Beloved (Song 8:5). The true way to be strong is to realize our weakness, and to feel that Christ must be all. The true way to grow in grace is to make use of Christ as a fountain for every minute's necessities. We ought to employ Him as the prophet's wife employed the oil – not only to pay our debts, but to live on also (2 Kgs. 4:7). We should strive to be able to say, 'The life I now live in the body, I live by faith in the Son of God, who loved me and gave himself for me' (Gal. 2:20).

I pity those who try to be holy without Christ! Your labour is all in vain. You are putting money in a bag with holes. You are pouring water into a sieve. You are rolling a huge round stone uphill. You are building up a wall with untempered mortar. Believe me, you are beginning at the wrong end. You must come to Christ first, and He shall give you His sanctifying Spirit. You must learn to say with Paul, 'I can do all this through him who gives me strength' (Phil. 4:13).

c) Christ is not only all in the sanctification of a true Christian – but all in his **comfort** in time present. A saved soul has many sorrows. He has a *body* like other men, weak and frail. He has a *heart* like other men, and often a more sensitive one too. He has *trials* and *losses* to bear like others, and often more. He has his share of bereavements, deaths, disappointments, crosses. He has ...

the world to oppose,

a place in life to fill blamelessly,

unconverted relatives to bear with patiently,

persecutions to endure,

and a death to die.

And who is sufficient for these things? What shall enable a believer to bear all this? Nothing but the consolation there is in Christ (Phil. 2:1).

Jesus is indeed the Brother born for adversity. He is the Friend that sticks closer than a brother, and He alone can comfort His people. He can be touched with the feeling of their infirmities, for He suffered Himself (Heb. 4:15). He knows what sorrow is, for He was a Man of sorrows. He knows what an aching body is, for His body was racked with pain. He cried, '... all my bones are out of joint' (Ps. 22:14). He knows what poverty and weariness are – for He was often wearied and had nowhere to lay His head. He knows what family unkindness is, for even His brethren did not believe Him. He had no honour in His own house.

And Jesus knows exactly how to comfort His afflicted people. He knows ...

how to pour oil and wine into the wounds of the spirit,

how to fill up gaps in empty hearts,

how to speak a word in season to the weary,

how to heal the broken heart,

how to make all our bed in sickness,

how to draw near when we are faint, and say, 'Fear not, I am your salvation' (see Lam. 3:57).

We talk of sympathy being pleasant. There is no sympathy like that of Christ. In all our afflictions, He is afflicted. He knows our sorrows. In all our pain, He is pained, and like the good physician, He will not measure out to us one drop of sorrow too much. David once said, 'When anxiety was great within me, your consolation brought me joy' (Ps. 94:19). Many a believer, I am sure, could say as much. 'If the Lord Himself had not stood by me, the deep waters would have gone over my soul' (see Ps. 124:1–5).

How a believer gets through all his troubles appears wonderful.

How he is carried through the fire and water he passes through seems past comprehension. But the true account of it is just this: that Christ is not only *justification* and *sanctification* but *consolation* also.

Oh, you who want unfailing comfort, I commend you to Christ! In Him alone there is *no failure*.

Rich men are disappointed in their treasures.

Learned men are disappointed in their books.

Husbands are disappointed in their wives.

Wives are disappointed in their husbands.

Parents are disappointed in their children.

Statesmen are disappointed when, after many a struggle, they attain place and power. They find out, to their cost, that it is more pain than pleasure, that it is disappointment, annoyance, incessant trouble, worry, vanity and vexation of spirit. But no man was ever disappointed in Christ.

d) But as Christ is all in the comforts of a true Christian in time present, so Christ is all in his *hopes* for time to come. Few men and women, I suppose, are to be found who do not indulge in hopes of some kind about their souls. But the hopes of the vast majority are nothing but *vain imaginations*. They are built on no solid foundation. No living man but the real child of God – the sincere, thorough-going Christian – can give a reasonable account of the hope that is in him. No hope is reasonable which is not scriptural.

A true Christian has a good hope when he looks forward; the worldly man has none. A true Christian sees light in the distance; the worldly man sees nothing but darkness. And what is the hope of a true Christian? It is just this – that Jesus Christ is ...

coming again,

coming without sin,

coming with all His people,

coming to wipe away every tear,

coming to raise His sleeping saints from the grave,

coming to gather together all His family, that they may be forever with Him.

Why is a believer *patient*? Because he looks for the coming of the Lord. He can bear hard things without murmuring. He knows the time is short. He waits quietly for the King.

Why is he *moderate* in all things? Because he expects his Lord soon to return. His treasure is in heaven, his good things are yet to come. The world is not his rest, but an inn; and an inn is not home. He knows that 'he who is coming will come and will not delay' (Heb. 10:37); Christ is coming, and that is enough.

This is indeed a 'blessed hope' (Titus 2:13)!

Now is the school-time – then the eternal holiday.

Now is the tossing on the waves of a troublesome world – then the quiet harbour.

Now is the scattering – then the gathering.

Now is the time of sowing – then the harvest.

Now is the working season – then the wages.

Now is the cross – then the crown.

People talk of their 'expectations' and hopes from this world. None have such solid expectations as a saved soul. He can say, 'My soul, wait ... only upon God; for my expectation is from him' (Ps. 62:5, KJV).

In all true saving religion Christ is ...

all in justification,

all in sanctification,

all in comfort,

all in hope.

Blessed is that mother's child that knows it, and far more blessed is he that feels it, too. Oh, that men would prove themselves, and see what they know of it for their own souls!

4. Christ will be all in heaven

I cannot dwell long on this point. I have not power, if I had space and room. I can ill describe things unseen and a world unknown. But this I know, that all men and women who reach heaven will find that even there also Christ is all.

Like the altar in Solomon's temple, Christ crucified will be the grand object in heaven. That altar struck the eye of everyone who entered the temple gates. It was a great bronze altar, twenty cubits broad, as broad as the front of the temple itself (2 Chr. 3:4; 4:1). So in like manner will Jesus fill the eyes of all who enter glory. In the midst of the throne, and surrounded by adoring angels and saints, there will be the Lamb that was slain. And the Lamb shall be the light of the place (Rev. 5:6; 21:23).

The *praise* of the Lord Jesus will be the eternal song of all the inhabitants of heaven. They will say with a loud voice, 'Worthy is the Lamb, who was slain'; 'To him who sits on the throne and to the Lamb be praise and honour and glory and power, for ever and ever!' (Rev. 5:12,13).

The *service* of the Lord Jesus will be one eternal occupation of all the inhabitants of heaven. We shall 'serve him day and night in his temple' (Rev. 7:15). Blessed is the thought that we shall at length attend on Him without distraction, and work for Him without weariness.

The *presence* of Christ Himself shall be one everlasting *enjoyment* of the inhabitants of heaven. We shall see His face, and hear His voice, and speak with Him as friend with friend (Rev. 22:4). Sweet is the thought that whoever may be missing at the marriage supper, the Master Himself will be there. His presence will satisfy all our desires (Ps. 17:15).

What a sweet and glorious *home* heaven will be to those who have loved the Lord Jesus Christ in sincerity! Here we live by faith in Him, and find peace, though we see Him not. There we shall see Him face to face, and find that He is altogether lovely. 'Better what the eye sees than the roving of the appetite' (Eccl. 6:9)!

But alas, how little fit for heaven are many who talk of going to heaven when they die, while they manifestly have no saving faith and no real acquaintance with Christ. You give Christ no honour here. You have no communion with Him. You do not love Him. Alas, what could you do in heaven? It would be no place for you. Its *joys* would be no joys for you. Its *happiness* would be a happiness into which you could not enter. Its *employments* would be a weariness and a burden to your heart. Oh, repent and change before it be too late!

I trust I have now shown how deep are the foundations of that little expression 'Christ is all'.

I might easily add to the things I have said, if space permitted. The subject is not exhausted. I have barely walked over the surface of it. There are mines of precious truth connected with it, which I have left unopened.

I might show how Christ ought to be all in a *visible church*.

Religious buildings, numerous religious services, gorgeous ceremonies, troops of ordained men – all, all are nothing in the sight of God, if the Lord Jesus Himself in all His offices is not honoured, magnified and exalted. That church is but a dead carcass in which Christ is not all.

I might show how Christ ought to be all in a *ministry*. The great work which ordained men are intended to do is to lift up Christ. We are to be like the pole on which the bronze serpent was hung. We are useful so long as we exalt the great object of faith – but useful no further. We are to be ambassadors to carry tidings to a rebellious world about the King's Son; and if we teach men to think more about us and our office than about Him, we are not fit for our place. The Spirit will never honour that minister who does not testify of Christ, who does not make Christ all.

I might show how language seems exhausted in the Bible, in describing Christ's various *offices*. I might describe how figures seem endless, which are employed in unfolding Christ's fullness. The High Priest, the Mediator, the Redeemer, the Saviour, the Advocate, the Shepherd, the Physician, the Bridegroom, the Head, the Bread of Life, the Light of the world, the Way, the Door, the Vine, the Rock, the Fountain, the Sun of Righteousness, the Forerunner, the Surety, the Captain, the Prince of life, the Amen, the Almighty, the Author and Finisher of faith, the Lamb of God, the King of saints, the Wonderful, the Mighty God, the Counsellor, the Bishop of souls – all these, and many more, are names given to Christ in Scripture. Each is a fountain of instruction and comfort for everyone who is willing to drink of it. Each supplies matter for useful meditation.

But I trust I have said enough to throw light on the point I want to impress on the minds of all who read this message. I trust I have said enough to show the immense importance of the *practical conclusions* with which I now desire to finish the subject.

1. Is Christ all? Then let us **learn the utter uselessness of a Christless religion.** There are only too many baptized men and women who practically know nothing at all about Christ. Their religion consists in a few vague notions and empty expressions. They 'trust they are no worse than others'. They 'keep to their church'. They 'try to do their duty'. They 'do nobody any harm'. They 'hope God will be merciful to them'. They 'trust the Almighty will pardon their sins, and take them to heaven when they die'. This is about the whole of their religion!

But what do these people *know practically* about Christ? Nothing, nothing at all! What *experimental acquaintance* have they with His offices and work, His blood, His righteousness, His mediation, His priesthood, His intercession? None, none at all! Ask them about a saving faith, ask them about being born again of the Spirit, ask them about being sanctified in Christ Jesus. What answer will you get? You are a barbarian to them! You have asked them simple Bible questions. But they know no more about them experimentally than a Buddhist or a Turk! And yet this is the religion of hundreds and thousands of people who are called Christians all over the world!

If any reader of this message is a man of this kind, I warn him plainly that such Christianity will never take him to heaven. It may do very well in the eye of man. It may pass muster very decently at the church meeting, in the place of business, or in the streets. But it will never comfort you. It will never satisfy your conscience. It will never save your soul.

I warn you plainly that all notions and theories about God being merciful without Christ, and excepting through Christ, are baseless *delusions and empty imaginations*. Such theories are as purely *an idol of man's invention* as the idol of Juggernaut. They are all of the earth, earthy. They never came down from heaven. The God of heaven has sealed and appointed Christ as the one only Saviour and way of life, and all who would be saved must be content to be saved by Him, or they will never be saved at all.

Let every reader take notice. I give you fair warning this day. A religion without Christ will never save your soul.

2. Let me say another thing. Is Christ all? Then **learn the enormous folly of joining anything with Christ in the matter of salvation.** There are multitudes of baptized men and women who profess to honour Christ – but in reality do Him great dishonour. They give Christ a certain place in their system of religion, but not the place which God intended Him to fill. Christ alone is not all in all to their souls. No! It is either Christ and the *church*, or Christ and the *sacraments*, or Christ and His *ordained ministers*, or Christ and their own *repentance*, or Christ and their own *goodness*, or Christ and their own *prayers*, or Christ and their own *sincerity* and *charity* on which they practically rest their souls.

If any reader of this message is a Christian of this kind, I warn him also plainly that his religion is an offence to God. You are changing God's plan of salvation into a plan of your own devising. You are in effect *deposing Christ from His throne* by giving the glory due to Him to another.

I care not who it is that teaches such religion, and on whose word you build. Whether he be pope or cardinal, archbishop or bishop, dean or archdeacon, presbyter or deacon, Episcopalian or Presbyterian, Baptist or Independent, Wesleyan or Plymouth brother, whoever adds anything to Christ teaches you wrong.

I care not what it is that you add to Christ. Whether it be the necessity of joining the church of Rome, or of being an Episcopalian, or of becoming a free churchman, or of giving up the liturgy, or of being dipped in baptism – whatever you may practically add to Christ in the matter of salvation, you do Christ an injury.

Take heed what you are doing. Beware of giving to Christ's *servants* the honour due to none but Christ. Beware of giving the Lord's *ordinances* the honour due unto the Lord. Beware of resting the burden of your soul on anything but Christ, and Christ alone.

3. Let me say another thing. Is Christ all? **Then let all who want to be saved apply direct to Christ.** There are many who hear of Christ with the ear and believe all they are told about Him. They allow that there is no salvation excepting in Christ. They acknowledge that Jesus alone can deliver them from hell, and present them faultless before God. But they seem never to get beyond this general acknowledgement. They never fairly lay hold on Christ for their own souls. They stick fast in a state of wishing and wanting and feeling and intending – and never get any further. They see what we mean; they know that it is all true. They hope one day to get the full benefit of it – but at present they get no benefit whatever. The *world* is their all. *Politics* are their all. *Pleasure* is their all. *Business* is their all. But Christ is not their all.

If any reader of this message is a man of this kind, I warn him also plainly, he is in a bad state of soul. You are as truly in the way to hell in your present condition as Judas Iscariot or Ahab or Cain! Believe me, there must be actual faith in Christ, or else Christ died in vain, so far as you are concerned. It is not looking at the bread which feeds the hungry man – but the actual eating of it. It is not gazing on the lifeboat which saves the shipwrecked sailor – but the actual getting into it. It is not knowing and believing that Christ is a Saviour which can save your soul, unless there are actual transactions between you and Christ. You must be able to say, 'Christ is my Saviour, because I have come to Him by faith, and taken Him for my own.' 'Much of religion,' said Luther, 'turns on being able to use *possessive pronouns*. Take from me the word "my," and you take from me God!'

Hear the advice I give you this day, and act upon it at once. Stand still no longer, waiting for some imaginary frames and feelings which will never come. Hesitate no longer under the idea that you must first of all obtain the Spirit, and then come to Christ. Arise and come to Christ just as you are. He waits for you, and is as *willing* to save as He is *mighty* to save. He is the appointed *Physician for sin-sick souls*. Deal with Him as you would with your doctor about the cure of a disease of your body. Make a direct application to Him and tell Him all your wants. Take with you words this day, and cry mightily to the Lord Jesus for pardon and peace, as the thief did on the cross. Do as that man did cry, 'Jesus, remember me' (Luke 23:42). Tell Him you have heard that He receives sinners, and that you are such. Tell Him you want to be saved, and ask Him to save you. Rest not until you have actually tasted for yourself that the Lord is gracious. Do this, and you shall find, sooner or later, if you are really in earnest – that Christ is all.

4. One more thing let me add. Is Christ all? Then **let all His converted people deal with Him as if they really believed it.** Let them lean on Him and trust Him far more than they have ever done yet. Alas, there are many of the Lord's people who live far below their privileges! There are many truly Christian souls who rob themselves of their own peace and forsake their own mercies. There are many who insensibly join their own faith, or the work of the Spirit in their own hearts, to Christ, and so miss the fullness of gospel peace. There are many who make little progress in their pursuit of holiness and shine with a very dim light. And why is all this? Simply because – in nineteen cases out of twenty – men do not make Christ all in all.

Now I call on every reader of this message who is a believer, I beseech him for his own sake, to make sure that Christ is really and thoroughly his all in all. Beware of allowing yourself to **mingle** anything of your own with Christ.

Have you faith? It is a priceless blessing. Happy indeed are they who are willing and ready to trust Jesus. But take heed you do not *make a Christ of your faith*. Rest not on your own faith – but on Christ.

Is the work of the Spirit in your soul? Thank God for it. It is a work that shall never be overthrown. But oh, beware lest, unawares to yourself, you make a Christ of the work of the Spirit! Rest not on the work of the Spirit – but on Christ.

Have you any inward feelings of religion, and experience of grace? Thank God for it. Thousands have no more religious feeling than a cat or dog! But oh, beware lest you make a Christ of your feelings and sensations! They are poor, uncertain things and sadly dependent on our bodies and outward circumstances. Rest not a grain of weight on your feelings. Rest only on Christ.

Learn, I entreat you, to look more and more at the great object of faith, Jesus Christ, and to keep your mind dwelling on Him. So doing you would find faith and all the other graces grow, though the growth at the time might be imperceptible to yourself. He who would prove a skilful archer must look not at the arrow – but at the mark.

Alas, I fear there is a great deal of pride and unbelief still sticking in the hearts of many believers! Few seem to realize how much they need a Saviour. Few seem to understand how thoroughly they are indebted to Him. Few seem to comprehend how much they need Him every day. Few seem to feel how simply and like a child they ought to hang their souls on Him. Few seem to be aware how full of *love* He is to His poor, weak people, and how ready to *help* them! And few therefore seem to know the peace and joy and strength and power to live a godly life, which is to be had in Christ.

Change your plan, reader, if your conscience tells you are guilty; change your plan, and learn to trust Christ more. *Physicians* love to see patients coming to consult them; it is their office to receive the sickly, and if possible to effect cures. The *advocate* loves to be employed; it is his calling. The *husband* loves his wife to trust him and lean upon him; it is his delight to cherish her and promote her comfort. And Christ loves His people ...

to *lean* on Him,

to *rest* in Him,

to *call* on Him,

to *abide* in Him.

Notes

William Shakespeare, *Hamlet*, Act I Scene V.

John Owen, *The Works of John Owen* Vol. 13 (Lenox, MA: HardPress Publishing, 2013).

Augustus Montague Toplady, 1740–78, 'Rock of Ages'.

Alexander Pope, 'An Essay on Man' (1734).

William Gurnall, *The Christian in Complete Armour* Vol. 1, Part Second, Direction 1 – First General Part (Edinburgh: The Banner of Truth Trust, 1986).

John Bunyan, *The Pilgrim's Progress* (quoted edition published London: Penguin, 1965, 1987).

TRUTHFORLIFE®

THE BIBLE-TEACHING MINISTRY OF **ALISTAIR BEGG**

The mission of Truth For Life is to teach the Bible with clarity and relevance so that unbelievers will be converted, believers will be established, and local churches will be strengthened.

Daily Program

Each day, Truth For Life distributes the Bible teaching of Alistair Begg across the U.S., in selected cities in Canada, and in several locations outside of the U.S. on over 1,700 radio outlets. To find a radio station near you, visit **truthforlife.org/station-finder**

Free Teaching

The daily program, and Truth For Life's entire teaching archive of over 2,000 Bible-teaching messages, can be accessed for free online and through Truth For Life's full-feature mobile app. A daily app is also available that provides direct access to the daily message and daily devotional. Download the free mobile apps at **truthforlife.org/app** and listen free online at **truthforlife.org.**

At-Cost Resources

Books and full-length teaching from Alistair Begg on CD, DVD and MP3CD are available for purchase *at cost, with no mark up*. Visit **truthforlife.org/store**

Where To Begin?

If you're new to Truth For Life and would like to know where to begin listening and learning, find starting point suggestions at **truthforlife.org/firststep.** For a full list of ways to connect with Truth For Life, visit **truthforlife.org/subscribe**

Contact Truth For Life

P.O. Box 398000 Cleveland, Ohio 44139
phone 1 (888) 588-7884   **email** letters@truthforlife.org
 /truthforlife   @truthforlife truthforlife.org

10Publishing is the publishing house of **10ofThose**.
It is committed to producing quality Christian
resources that are biblical and accessible.

www.10ofthose.com is our online retail arm selling
thousands of quality books at discounted prices.

For information contact: **sales@10ofthose.com**
or check out our website: **www.10ofthose.com**